"*A Story Worth Living* is a deeply honest invitation to step out of hiding and into healing. Amy Loflin writes with both tenderness and truth, guiding women back to the heart of God and the purpose He planted in them long ago."

—**Angela Thomas Pharr,**
Author and Speaker

a story WORTH Living

Reclaim your Confidence, Purpose, and Peace

AMY LOFLIN

LUCIDBOOKS

A Story Worth Living: Reclaim your Confidence, Purpose, and Peace

Published by Lucid Books in Houston, TX
www.LucidBooks.com

ISBN: 978-1-63296-854-8
eISBN: 978-1-63296-855-5

Special Sales: Most Lucid Books titles are available in special quantity discounts. Custom imprinting or excerpting can also be done to fit special needs. Contact Lucid Books at Info@LucidBooks.com

To the woman who reached for Jesus over 2,000 years ago—your bold faith still echoes through time.

And to every woman who follows in her footsteps, refuses to stay hidden, and reaches for more, may God bless your deliberate pursuit of Jesus.

May you continue to walk with Him, rooted in grace and courage as you pen a story worth living.

This book is for you.

Contents

Part Four: Take Another Seat

Part Five: The New

Preface

This book began as something personal, well before it ever became something public.

A few years ago, I hit a spiritual plateau. I was doing "all the right things." I was in consistent prayer, part of a faith-filled community, and serving others. But deep down, I felt a holy restlessness I couldn't ignore. I sensed God was calling me to something deeper.

Hebrews 12:1–2 (NIV) echoed in my spirit: "Let us throw off everything that hinders . . . fixing our eyes on Jesus." I began to wonder what blindspots, lingering misconceptions, and unhealed wounds were quietly hindering me. I knew I had to trust Jesus enough to show me what I was carrying and be willing to surrender it. I wanted to be free from the insecurities, masks, and fears I had unknowingly carried for years. I was ready to become my most authentic self, the woman He created me to be.

I also understood that I didn't want to just know more about Jesus. I hungered to encounter Him. I longed to sit with His words and His presence in a way I hadn't before. So I slowed down. I chose a handful of stories where Jesus met people face to face and let those moments become sacred space for my own healing and growth. I marinated in them and asked, "What do You want to show me here? How do You want me to respond?"

What began as a personal pilgrimage became a season of transformation. Jesus became more real to me than ever before. And while I didn't know it at the time, He was planting the seeds for this book. It's not just a reflection of my journey but a tool for yours. I wrote it because I know what it's like to need gentle reminders that you're not too far gone, too broken, or too late. I know what it's like to need someone to say, "I've been there too."

So before I ever imagined you, the reader, I had to face this story myself. And as you read, I believe you'll find a piece of your own story here too.

Introduction

Wherever this book finds you—tired, hopeful, curious, or hurting—I want you to know I see you. In the midst of your daily hustle, you're pouring yourself into being everything for everyone. You're juggling deadlines, caring for aging parents, and guiding your kids as they grow up way too fast. With the demands of life, your faith feels more like a checkbox than a living, breathing identity. You're craving a deeper connection with God, but the thought of adding one more thing to your overflowing plate feels overwhelming.

If it seems like I have an all-access pass to your heart's longings, it's because I've been there too. I know the weight of being overwhelmed and the deep ache for peace, purpose, and connection. In our quiet moments of doubt and anxiety, we all yearn for healing and clarity. We long to live a meaningful life—a life where we're proud of the legacy we will one day leave behind. We want to walk confidently in our purpose, free from the obstacles holding us back from becoming the woman God created and called us to be.

What if following Jesus isn't just another task, but the answer to your soul's deepest longing?

This is a question that stirred something in me, not just as a writer but as a woman craving more from her own faith. That's why I'm so excited this book is in your hands. You are about to engage in a story from Scripture that has profoundly impacted my life. And I pray it offers you the same hope, healing, and clarity.

The story in the Bible of the woman who reached out to touch the hem of Jesus's garment isn't just a historical event. It is a story that speaks to the heart of every woman. It's about reaching out in faith to Jesus when you've been hurt, hidden, or drifting, and finding the healing and love you never thought possible.

On the pages ahead, you'll step into this woman's shoes, feel what she felt, and witness her transformation through the lens of your own heart. Together, we'll explore the cultural, emotional, and spiritual context of her encounter with Jesus and reflect on the ways this story might echo in your own life.

This work is an invitation to uncover the hidden parts of your heart, whether it's shame, labels, or habits, which may have kept you from fully stepping into your calling. You'll encounter the healing power of Jesus and discover how this transformative story can guide you toward freedom, peace, and a life of purpose.

As you turn these pages, I encourage you to do so with an open heart. Allow yourself to reflect deeply, ask the hard questions, and receive God's direction and insight for you. This book isn't just a story to read; it's a story to live. With each section, choose to reflect, journal, and make the powerful truths of this story your own. This journey is not just about reading; it's about transforming your heart.

Getting the Most Out of This Book

We begin this experience by immersing ourselves in a specific New Testament story, an encounter Jesus had with a woman. As we focus deeply on one story, you may be surprised at how much Jesus reveals when you spend this deliberate, sacred time with Him. There is always more beneath the surface, and discovering the deeper gems takes time and intentionality. We will walk through her story together, but the Holy Spirit is your guide.

The Holy Spirit is the One who will meet you in these pages, whispering new truths, calling you forward, and strengthening your faith one step at a time. Whether this story is familiar or new, I invite you to sit with it like never before. Let go of what you already know and lean in with expectation because Jesus always has more to reveal.

Each chapter will guide you through one small step—one revelation, one moment of reflection, one invitation—to trust a little more. And just like the woman in this story, these small steps taken with Jesus will lead to something greater—a deeper faith, a transformed heart, a life more fully surrendered. This process is how small steps lead to big faith.

Before fully grasping how this story applies today, we must step into that original, historical world. Too often, we rush to apply Jesus's teachings without first pausing to understand Him—who He was in His time, how He spoke, and what His words meant to those who first heard them.

When we look at those things, we are more equipped to unpack the story and discover the transferable principles and universal truths we can embrace today. Through this experience, you will learn some of the cultural nuances of the era and their significance to the original audience, the things we may otherwise miss with our 21st century lens. When you combine the historical context with what the Holy Spirit reveals to you through reading, prayer, and journaling, you'll find yourself challenged to break open the box you may not have even realized was limiting your view of Jesus.

The Bible is unlike any other book and should be approached in a way that's equally unique. Many of us have been taught to read for information or entertainment. But when it comes to Scripture, the goal is different. The Bible isn't just a source of facts; it's meant to shape us. As you read, aim to engage with it in a way that leads to greater self-awareness and real-life change. You're not only gathering information; you're inviting transformation.

Throughout this book, you'll find Reflect & Respond sections designed to guide you on this journey. These journaling prompts will help you process your reading and uncover deeper meaning. They'll encourage you to reflect on your reactions and explore how the story speaks to your life. You'll discover timeless principles to deepen your relationship with Jesus and better understand yourself.

The key to transformation lies in the practice of reflection and listening. Journaling isn't about "getting it right;" it's about being real. It's about showing up, listening, and allowing Jesus to meet you where you are. Whether you're a seasoned journaler or this is your first time, approach it with an open heart. There's no right or wrong way to do it. You can write in short phrases, create mind maps, note keywords, or even sketch. If you're unsure what to write, start by rewriting the prompt, and you may be surprised how the words flow once you begin. Remember, this is your time to explore and discover. There's no pressure, no judgment. No one will grade you. This journal is yours alone. It's a sacred space for reflection, growth, and discovery. If you're craving a deeper journaling experience, visit www.echojoycollective.com for free bonus material and printable tools designed to help you linger longer in the presence of God.

You could choose to simply read this book and have a good experience. But if you're seeking true transformation, I urge you to prioritize active prayer and reflection time. The insights, reflections, and revelations that will make this journey impactful don't come from my words alone; they come from the time you spend with Jesus as you process your reading. The more you pour in, the more you'll receive. Guaranteed.

Part One

The Story

"Spiritual reading is not only reading about spiritual people or spiritual things. It is also reading spiritually, that is, in a spiritual way. Reading in a spiritual way is reading with a desire to let God come closer to us.

The purpose of spiritual reading is not to master knowledge or information but to let God's Spirit master us. Strange as it may sound, spiritual reading means to let ourselves be read by God.

Spiritual reading is reading with an inner attentiveness to the movement of God's Spirit in our outer and inner lives. With that attentiveness, we will allow God to read us and to explain to us what we are truly about."

—Henri J. M. Nouwen

Nouwen, Henri J. M. *You Are the Beloved: Daily Meditations for Spiritual Living*. Convergent Books, 2017, p. 25.

Chapter One

Priming the Heart

Can you feel it? The buzz of anticipation? You are about to step into a story that the greatest storyteller and story maker, Jesus Himself, began centuries ago. This isn't just history; it's an invitation—your invitation.

Before we begin, take a deep breath. Settle your heart. Step away from the noise. Ask God to prepare you for what He wants to reveal through this journey. As you read through the following message, hear His voice calling you with tender attention. (I can understand and appreciate how difficult it may feel to read words a human has written from the viewpoint of God. It feels delicate to me, too, as the writer. Please note that this is my interpretation formed from my finite knowledge of Scripture, personal experiences, and spiritual understanding of what a good and loving Heavenly Father would say to His cherished daughter.)

My Beloved,

I am so happy to spend this time with you. I've been looking forward to this since the moment I created you. When I walked this earth and had the encounter you're about to read, I knew this story would one day make its way into your hands. It brings Me great joy to walk this journey with you.

During this time together, I want to show you more of My love. It is deeper, truer, more powerful than you have imagined. I want to shatter the misconceptions that have kept you distant from Me and break the chains that have held you back.

My beloved, I am here to set you free.

So will you trust Me? Place your hand in Mine. Let's walk this together. Lay aside distractions, burdens, and fears. Just be with Me. I am your safe place, your refuge. My hands are mighty yet tender. You can trust Me.

I've been waiting for you. And I'm not going anywhere.

Reflect & Respond

Pause for a moment. Let His words settle in. Close your eyes, take a few deep, cleansing breaths, and observe what stirs within you. Notice your heart's response to His call. Do you feel warmth? Resistance? Hesitation? Perhaps longing? Whatever it is, bring it to Him. There is no right or wrong way to respond. Just be real.

PRAYER

Dear God,

You already know my heart and the fears and doubts that have caused me to keep You at arm's length. I want to trust You and follow You, but sometimes I struggle. Help my unbelief. Yet even in my hesitation, I long to know You more. Please fan the flame of anticipation You've sparked in me as I place my hand in Yours.

Continue in prayer, taking all the time you need.

Scripture

Step into the scene that will be our focus throughout this book. You might want to use your Bible or an app to explore other versions or translations to gain more understanding.

Through our journey, we will reference the story as written by Luke.

On the other side of the lake, the crowds welcomed Jesus because they had been waiting for him. Then a man named Jairus, a leader of the local synagogue, came and fell at Jesus' feet, pleading with him to come home with him. His only daughter, who was about twelve years old, was dying.

As Jesus went with him, he was surrounded by the crowds. A woman in the crowd had suffered for twelve years with constant bleeding, and she could find no cure. Coming up behind Jesus, she touched the fringe of his robe. Immediately, the bleeding stopped.

"Who touched me?" Jesus asked.

Everyone denied it, and Peter said, "Master, this whole crowd is pressing up against you."

But Jesus said, "Someone deliberately touched me, for I felt healing power go out from me." When the woman realized that she could not stay hidden, she began to tremble and fell to her knees in front of him. The whole crowd heard her explain why she had touched him and that she had been immediately healed. "Daughter," he said to her, "your faith has made you well. Go in peace."

—Luke 8:40–48

She had suffered a great deal from many doctors and over the years had spent everything she had to pay them. But she had gotten no better. In fact, she had gotten worse.

—Mark 5:26

Reflect & Respond

Before we dive deeper into this scene, take a moment to process what you've read. Whether this is your first time reading this story or the hundredth, reflect on your initial reactions. Highlight, circle, or journal words and phrases that stand out to you. Without overthinking it, record one thing that stands out to you in each of these areas:

- Something important
- Something confusing
- Something surprising

Historical Context

Reflecting on Luke's account, we must step into this woman's world and consider her cultural and religious realities to fully grasp the weight of her story. This deeper understanding helps us appreciate the radical nature and multiple layers of her encounter with Jesus.

Jewish Law, often called the Mosaic Law, was a set of religious and cultural guidelines God gave the people of Israel through His prophet Moses. It governed every aspect of daily life—worship, diet, relationships, cleanliness—to help the Israelites live set apart as God's holy people. Specific regulations around purity were central to these laws. A woman who was menstruating, for example, was considered ceremonially unclean. It wasn't a moral judgment but part of a broader symbolic system to reflect holiness and separation.

During menstruation, a woman could not participate in worship or certain community activities, thereby creating physical and spiritual barriers she could not cross. Anyone who touched her would also be considered unclean and required to wait until evening and bathe before they could rejoin community life. This uncleanness even extended to anything she sat on or laid on. Touching those items would also make someone unclean (Lev. 15:19–22).

When her bleeding ended, she was required to undergo a purification process. This involved a waiting period of seven days after bathing, and then, on the eighth day, she would bring a sacrifice to the temple to complete her purification (Lev. 15:28–30).

These laws extended beyond hygiene regulations; they were deeply tied to a person's spiritual and social identity. To be unclean was to be excluded. The Law required anyone in an unclean state to be cut off from the assembly to protect the holiness of the temple and its worship (Num. 19:20). Anything or anyone touched by an unclean person became defiled as well, widening the circle of separation (Num. 19:22).

The Mosaic Law held deep significance for the Jewish people. It was the foundation of their faith, identity, and community. It wasn't simply a rule book; it was a sacred covenant. While modern cultures often view laws as flexible or open to interpretation, the Mosaic Law was revered as holy, unchangeable, and binding.

The Mosaic Law held deep significance for the Jewish people. It was the foundation of their faith, identity, and community. It wasn't simply a rule book; it was a sacred covenant.

With this cultural lens, we see the woman's encounter with Jesus in a new light. She wasn't just sick; she was isolated. The system meant to guide and protect had become a source of deep loneliness and shame for her. After 12 years of bleeding, she probably had no support system. She may have viewed her body as broken and her soul unworthy. Her spiritual life was likely as anemic as her body, and her future must have felt hopeless and unbearably lonely.

Now let's step into her story in a more personal way. Imagine what it must have felt like to carry that burden—12 years of suffering, longing, and courage. In the next chapter, we'll enter the scene from her perspective and walk with her through her desperation, her risk, and the moment everything changed.

Chapter Two

Through Her Eyes

We have gathered the facts and examined this encounter through a historical and cultural lens. Now it's time to shift gears. Understanding the stories of the Bible requires both the mind and the heart, engaging not only with knowledge but with an openness to what God may reveal beneath the surface.

The following narrative invites you into the story through the eyes of the woman who reached for Jesus. Using Luke's account as the foundation, I have expanded on her experience, weaving in the emotions, thoughts, and struggles she may have carried after 12 years of suffering. Read it slowly. Let yourself feel her desperation, her longing, and her courage. Notice your own thoughts and emotions as you journey through her story.

I have taken intentional creative liberties to bring this scene to life, guided by Scripture, prayer, and cultural context. My hope is that this expanded perspective deepens your connection to her story and ultimately to the multiple truths waiting to be uncovered.

Let's see this moment unfold through her eyes.

Her Narrative

I am weary. Just so weary. The shame and isolation define me. I've tried. Lord knows I've tried. I've spent all my money on doctors, each time hoping and praying this person can help me. Maybe this time I will be healed and set free. But no. Every time I've gotten my hopes up, they only come crashing down again. The emotional whirlwind is exhausting. The medical procedures they performed on my body only made the bleeding worse, and the doctors' expressions only made me feel smaller and dirtier. I've also sought healing from priests but with no luck. I was told my sin was too great and my faith was too small. Or perhaps my parents' sin created my condition. Some tried to command the bleeding to stop as if I were demon-possessed. Am I demon-possessed? Sometimes I wonder.

For 12 long years, the bleeding has refused to stop. So I know I am beyond healing. I am resigned to this life. No man will have me. I am cursed, tainted, foul, and broken. I can't blame them. No one would choose this life. The isolation slowly kills me. I try not to look at the other women, but for some reason, I can't tear my gaze away. I see them in the marketplace, walking in groups to the well, laughing and connecting.

They seem so carefree as they walk along, talking to whomever they choose. Of course, they never choose to talk to me. They look at me with disdain, sneering in my direction, talking and laughing about me. I am beneath them. Some days I want to yell and scream. But mostly I just want to slip into the shadows. It's strange. I hate it when they look at me like I'm garbage, but what's worse is when no one looks at me at all. Then my value is even smaller, not even worth acknowledging. There is an emptiness, a void in my soul. Am I even still alive? If a tree falls in the woods and no one hears it, does it make a sound? If a person walks past a crowd and no one sees her, is she still alive?

I remember going to the temple when I was a child. It was a confusing place. I was told God lives there. How did He get in there? Only the high priest is allowed to go into the holiest room where God resides. I've wondered at times what would happen if I snuck in there. Would God heal me? Would he kill me? Either would be fine with me.

The irony isn't lost on me. I see the people going to the festivals, to the temple. They have to buy an animal to sacrifice. This is to appease God, their way of telling him they are sorry for their sin. An animal must die and bleed. The blood of an unblemished, perfect animal is used to wash away the sins of the person making the offering. And yet here I am, a blemished woman who can't stop bleeding long enough to be considered clean in order to be able to approach the temple to offer a sacrifice. Is this a cruel joke? The Law was written in Leviticus that a bleeding woman was unclean and had to have seven full days free of bleeding before she could go to the pool to wash in a cleansing ceremony to no longer be considered unclean. I just cannot win in this system.

So I'm done. I will never allow myself to dare to hope again. I will never again trust a man of God. God has forgotten me. I am resigned to a life of isolation. I am building a wall of protection around what's left of my heart until—until I started hearing of a man named Jesus. I have heard he is a man of God, which makes me trust him even less. If there is a God, he certainly does not care about me. The priest made that clear. So no. I want nothing to do with this man, Jesus.

And yet as I am begging on the side of the road, I overhear the conversations of those heading to the lakeside. Somehow, they knew Jesus was on his way to our city. I watch as crowds of people abandon daily tasks and gather at the shore to welcome him. I catch pieces of phrases in the air. "He teaches like no other." "He eats with sinners." "He healed a paralyzed man." "He allows and even encourages women to follow him." "He raised a widow's son from the dead." "He's different." "I heard he is the Messiah!"

I don't make a formal decision because I know if I were being rational, I would remain on my spot by the road. And yet I find myself rising and walking along with the crowd. This crowd of people seems to take on a new energy. The excitement is so distracting that no one notices I slipped in among them. Otherwise, I would surely be yelled at to remove my contamination from the crowd. So I allow myself to be drawn in. The excitement and anticipation of the crowd grows as someone shouts. They can see the boat approaching. The murmurs of the crowd intensify, and I stand on my tiptoes. Sure enough, I watch as a boat slowly comes ashore.

I don't know which one is Jesus at first. As the men disembark, they all seem so ordinary. Although Jesus is not dressed as a priest, it becomes clear which one he is. He carries an authority without saying a word, and I suddenly feel emboldened in his presence. I don't know how to explain it, but I feel drawn to him. Every man I have ever put my trust in has shamed, hurt, dismissed, and used me. Yet at this moment, I need to be near this man.

I am so close. I inhale to call out his name, but someone else—Jairus—does it first. I recognize him. Everyone knows him. He is a leader in our local temple. As I clamp my mouth shut, I am surprised to see what unfolds before me and the crowd. Jairus falls to his knees in front of Jesus. This man of great power, a leader in our community, a man who worships the Jewish God, is falling at the feet of this man. Tears stream down his face. What will the other religious leaders say, the ones who remained piously behind in the temple? I can't believe this man's audacity, his risk. Doesn't he know he could lose his position with this one act? He begs Jesus to come to his home to save his daughter who is dying. And the crowd follows as Jesus begins to walk with Jairus.

My powerful, undeniable, unavoidable desire to be near Jesus remains. The crowd fades in my vision and hearing, and I am laser-focused on his back. I'm being pulled toward him; there is no other way to explain it. An unseen force propels me, something beyond my own will. I am merely captivated, surrendered. I suddenly find myself right behind him. The crowd is packed tightly. Others are curious and drawn to him, so I know my chance is fleeting. Perhaps the boldness of Jairus inspired me. Perhaps there is still a glimmer of hope of healing that propels me. But it's more than that.

My motivation is greater than my physical sickness. I just want him. So I do it. My hand suddenly floats away from my side and reaches. My fingers brush against the fringe of his robe.

And time stands still.

Physically, it is only the lightest touch, like a moth to a flame, like wings whispering. Three of my fingertips casually, delicately brush along a couple of inches of fabric. But spiritually, it feels like worlds colliding. As if struck by lightning, I feel a jolt that begins in my fingertips and quickly spreads through every inch of my body. I know I am instantly new—instantly whole.

And then Jesus stops. He turns and asks, "Who touched me?" His question is so sudden and so bold, not angry but urgent. I freeze. Everyone is looking around, confused. They don't understand this question, but I do. There's a hush as Jesus surveys the crowd, and I slink back. One of his disciples tries to explain the situation by pointing out that many in the crowd were pressing in on him. I hold my breath, hoping this will be the end of it and Jesus will resume the processional to Jairus's home.

But instead, Jesus presses the issue. "Someone deliberately touched me, for I felt healing power go out of me." The crowd, curious, begins to murmur and look around. I witness shrugging shoulders and heads shaking in denial. I begin to tremble. As seconds tick by, my nerves are on fire. And when I dare to glance his way, Jesus's eyes are on mine. He knows it's me! Of course he does.

Without saying a word, I know what he wants. I suddenly understand why he refuses to drop the subject. He wants my voice to be heard; he wants my story to be shared. I take a step forward, trembling uncontrollably. I can't hold myself up. All eyes are on me as I collapse to my knees in front of Jesus. I am unsure if I can trust my voice. Then I lift my chin and gaze into the face of God. Immediately, I know Jesus is "the One." He is the Messiah! His eyes flood my soul with His compassion. It overwhelms me. The love in His expression is the greatest thing I have ever seen in my life. It is greater than any sunrise or rainbow. It is both personal and intimate, yet it isn't selective or elite. I feel completely seen, and it is beautiful. There is no disgust or judgment as I have been so accustomed to. There is only love in its purest form.

> He wants my voice to be heard; he wants my story to be shared.

His love has given me a voice, and I begin to speak. I share my story, the truths about myself I had always kept hidden at any cost, tucked beneath a blanket of shame. As tears flow, I explain my 12 years of suffering and try to put into words what just happened. My eyes lock on Jesus's loving gaze. The crowd is silent as I explain my miraculous healing. His face illuminates into a smile as His tender voice exclaims, "Daughter, your faith has made you well. Go in peace."

This is the most real, true experience of my life. But it also feels like a dream, too good to be true. I am in a daze as a messenger approaches and delivers news that Jairus's daughter has died.

Jesus breaks His eye contact with me, directing His attention to the new crisis. The crowd loses interest in me as they turn to follow Jesus to the home of Jairus. My eyes lock in on His cloak until I see it no longer. His words echo through my heart and mind, leaving a tattoo on my soul.

Daughter. He called me daughter. I have been called many things over the past 12 years, and all those labels cut me like a knife. I accepted them. I believed I was who the people said I was—trash, dirty, sinner, unworthy, disgusting, broken, a contagion to be isolated. No one would ever want to associate with me as it would only hinder their reputation. I wasn't worth the risk.

And yet Jesus calls me daughter! I wouldn't believe it if I didn't witness this firsthand. I wouldn't believe it if the title from His lips wasn't accompanied by a voice and a countenance full of compassion and tenderness that felt foreign yet like home. Just as Jesus knew my touch to His cloak was deliberate, I knew His words to me were deliberate, purposeful, and intentional. By calling me daughter, He was claiming me as His own. I am His. I am a daughter of the Son of God! At this, I weep right there on the ground. From this day forward, no matter what my future may hold, I will no longer wear the titles that once held me captive. I am royal, claimed, and forever a member of God's family. I will hold my chin up with confidence, knowing I am loved, worthy, and valued. I am His! I will never be the same.

By calling me daughter, He was claiming me as His own. I am His.

PRAYER

Dear God,

Thank You for this opportunity to engage with this encounter in a fresh and personal way. Open my heart and expand my mind as I begin to process this with You.

In Jesus's name, amen.

Reflect & Respond

Before moving forward, take a moment to sit with this story. Let it settle in your heart as you reflect on the thoughts and emotions it stirred within you. You've now stepped into this woman's world and felt her desperation, her hope, and her redemption. Without overanalyzing, reflect, pray, and journal your initial response to her narrative. Here are a few questions to consider:

- How do you see yourself in her?
- What emotions did this reading stir in you?
- How does your story intersect with hers?

Chapter Three

The Power of Focus

In the stillness of an early morning on a Hawaiian mountain, my husband and I stood at the top of Haleakalā. The air was crisp and cool, and the sky was painted with the first light of dawn. We were about to embark on an unforgettable adventure, a bike ride down the side of this towering volcano over 10,000 feet above sea level, with sweeping island views. I was thrilled to experience it, eager for the ride, and convinced it would be like the old saying, "It's like riding a bike." How hard could it be?

As we began our descent, the scope of the tour came into view, and fear seeped in—the sharp turns, the steep drop-offs, the twisting roads. It all suddenly seemed too much. I imagined myself tumbling down the mountain, bruised and scraped. So I did what any sane person would do. I rode the brakes. I went down the mountain like an old woman on a motorized scooter with a low battery. I didn't worry about the other riders, even as the distance between me and those ahead stretched farther and farther. Eventually, the guide pulled over, and all his ducklings followed suit. I admit I was a wee bit embarrassed when he came right over to me.

Fortunately, he was patient with me. "Amy, you're looking down, right in front of your tire. You need to look several feet ahead into the curve you're approaching. Your body will follow where your eyes are fixed."

Determined to make the most of this experience, I decided to apply his advice. I lifted my chin and forced my eyes forward. Approaching the next curve, I focused on where I wanted to go. Soon, I relaxed and kept up with the rest of the group. My confidence grew, and the bike ride that once felt daunting became a thrilling adventure.

> "Your body will follow where your eyes are fixed."

The guide's words stuck with me long after the excursion ended. "Your body will follow where your eyes are fixed." It quickly became clear that this wasn't just cycling advice—it was life advice. When my focus is consumed by fear, self-doubt, or past failures, I find myself stuck and unable to move forward. When my chin is tucked, I will always lag behind. But when I set my gaze on where I want to go, when I focus on the truth of where Jesus is leading me, my actions follow.

We see this concept on display in our Bible story. Take a look at our woman and pay attention to her gaze at different moments within the scene. At first, her gaze is downcast, likely focused on her seemingly insurmountable circumstances. We can imagine her consumed with self-pity, only seeing the unfairness of life and the pain the world has inflicted on her. Then we see her chin lift and her feet begin to move. She catches glimpses of Jesus, and something begins to shift in her mindset. Hope, wonder, and curiosity paint a bull's-eye on Jesus's cloak. Her gaze is laser-focused, and her body follows where her eyes are fixed.

The same can be true for you.

This marks a significant point on your journey and in this book. A shift is underway. From this moment forward, you're stepping into a powerful process of growth. Just like I had to lift my eyes and release the brake, you'll be invited to loosen your grip on what's holding you back. The journey may still have sharp turns and steep stretches, but you don't have to white-knuckle through it.

Just as my distractions became obstacles on that bike ride, your spiritual path will face detours, subtle ones that come disguised as everyday life.

Consider these words from the author of Hebrews: "Let us strip off every weight that slows us down, especially the sin that so easily trips us up. And let us run with endurance the race God has set before us. We do this by keeping our eyes on Jesus, the champion who initiates and perfects our faith" (Heb. 12:1–2).

What are your "weights" that need to be removed? What are the distractions in your life that make it difficult to follow Jesus? Maybe it's busyness, fatigue, anxiety, or the pull of perfectionism. Pausing to name them and raising your awareness can help you plan ways to avoid them or lessen their power.

Set up your journey for success. That might look like setting aside a specific time each day for reading, prayer, and journaling. Find a rhythm that allows you to engage with the material and listen for God's voice. You may even choose a designated spot in your home—a quiet corner where your Bible, book, pen, and journal wait to welcome you. Let it become a sacred place, a gentle reminder to focus your gaze.

Consider inviting someone on the journey, a trusted friend or mentor who can encourage you when distractions arise and gently hold you accountable. Or ask a small group to participate with you and discuss your reflections. Download a free small group facilitator guide at www.echojoy-collective.com. It includes tips and encouragement to help you host with confidence. Community sharpens focus and strengthens resolve.

And the best part? You won't run this race alone. The Holy Spirit is your guide, strength, and steady companion. With each step, you can set your intentions and focus on the One who already sees the finish line. This is where your stride changes.

So lift your chin, friend. A beautiful stretch of road lies ahead, and Jesus is already calling you forward. Keep your eyes on Him, and trust that your steps will follow.

PRAYER

Dear God,

Help me lift my eyes and fix them on You. I want to make the most of this book and our time together. When distractions pull at my attention or fear whispers in my ear, remind me that You are steady and near. Teach me to trust You with every turn of the page. Strengthen my focus, and let my steps follow where You lead. Thank You for being my constant guide.

In Jesus's name, amen.

Reflect & Respond

Where is your gaze focused? What are the distractions in your life that pull your attention away from Jesus, especially during your quiet time with Him?

How can you actively refocus your eyes on Jesus when those distractions arise? What specific practices or habits are you going to put in place to keep your gaze fixed on Him?

Who is someone you trust who can help you stay accountable as you focus on Jesus through this experience? How can they help you stay on track?

Moving forward, we will carefully examine some powerful components of this woman's story, drawing out lessons and insights we can apply to our lives. Each chapter will unpack a layer of her experience, reflecting on her pain, healing, and the transformative power of encountering Jesus. Through these reflections, you'll observe and become part of her story, seeing her truths as your own and discovering what Jesus has to reveal to you. With each step, you will draw closer to understanding the depth of His love and the power of His touch in your life.

Part Two

The Before

Before this woman's healing, there was heartache. Before the crowd, there was isolation. In the following chapters, we'll enter her world to understand and connect with her pain. Before we talk about the miracle, we must make room for the messy middle—the before. We'll explore what it was like for her to live under the crushing weight of life's circumstances.

Her story may sound ancient, but the ache is familiar. As we walk through her waiting, you may begin to recognize your similar heartaches.

Chapter Four

The Weight of Shame

(Note: This chapter contains a brief personal reflection on childhood abuse. If this is a sensitive area for you, please feel free to pause, skip, or take care in how you engage with this chapter.)

Shame is an intense force. It isolates, condemns, and suffocates. Before encountering Jesus, the bleeding woman is defined by shame. Picture her for a moment, seated on the dusty road, her body curled inward. Her shoulders sag, her chin is tucked against her chest as if she's shrinking beneath an invisible weight pressing on her. Every disapproving glance from a stranger adds another layer of silence and isolation. Her sickness is not just in her body; it has consumed her heart, making it impossible to believe she has anything left worth redeeming. For 12 years she has suffered from physical affliction and societal shame that marked her as unclean.

For a variety of reasons, I can see myself in our friend by the road. Sadly, shame is likely part of your story too. Sometimes the weight can be overwhelming. Shame isn't an easy topic to address, but we can do this. There is healing waiting on the other side.

Shame is incredibly powerful, and it's not always publicly visible as it was with this woman who encountered Jesus. It's often hidden deep inside, shielded behind a mask of busyness. We smile, show up, move on, and all the while shame whispers, "If they only knew what you've done. If they actually knew the real you, they'd want nothing to do with you." It steals our thoughts, our identity, and our authenticity. Shame taunts and consumes us, casting a shadow over the positive contributions we've made to the world.

> Shame taunts and consumes us, casting a shadow over the positive contributions we've made to the world.

Unfortunately, pain and shame can often be a byproduct of someone else's actions. Sometimes words or behaviors, whether intentional or not, are wielded to wound another. This kind of pain doesn't fade away with time. It becomes a scar, a lingering reminder that refuses to heal. It's a constant ache, a weight that pulls at your chest and clouds your ability to trust others and yourself. Shame breeds bitterness, like a weed that quietly takes root in the soul, growing deep and suffocating. It clouds your vision, distorting how you see the world and your place in it.

I know the weight of shame, the kind that clings to you, unrelenting like a second skin. I know how it can linger for years, buried beneath the surface, threatening to choke out your life. When I was five years old, someone my parents trusted to care for me betrayed that trust in the worst possible way. Sexual abuse is a violation that hurts and distorts everything you know about safety, love, and who you are.

That early trauma stole more than my innocence. It robbed me of my sense of self. As I grew older, the memories didn't stay in the past; they haunted me. They played on repeat, uninvited, in the quiet hours of the night. Even as years passed, I remained that little girl, trapped in the darkness of her pain. I felt dirty, violated, broken. And sometimes I wondered if I was beyond repair, ruined and unworthy of anything good.

Healing didn't come quickly. Forgiveness didn't come easily. But renewal first appeared the moment I allowed Light into the darkness. The process began in high school with a small, courageous step—speaking up. I turned to my parents, opened wounds I knew would hurt them, too, and admitted my struggle. That moment felt like tearing open a floodgate with a rush of emotion and pain. But it was also the start of hope. My parents didn't hesitate to find me a counselor, and suddenly the weight of my shame didn't feel so isolating anymore.

Trust, too, was built slowly. I met my husband, Chad, in college. He was patient, offering me the intentional care

I didn't think I deserved. Each step, each small act of kindness, reminded me I wasn't unlovable. I was worthy of a healthy, safe relationship.

But the true turning point came when I leaned into my relationship with Jesus. Time and again, I felt His presence—not as a distant, abstract idea but as a real, living connection to redeem even the most broken parts of me. Jesus didn't just heal me. He redeemed my story, weaving beauty into the fabric of my pain. He didn't rush my process but gently guided me toward forgiveness and wholeness, even when it felt impossible.

Jesus didn't just heal me. He redeemed my story, weaving beauty into the fabric of my pain.

In the quiet moments of my journey, when the past tried to reclaim me, the Spirit of Jesus whispered hope into the pain. His love wasn't a quick fix but a steady, unwavering force through the darkness. It's not that the scars disappeared; they didn't. But shame lost its grip on me. My past no longer defined me. Jesus redeemed both my story and my future, renaming my scars as trophies of His grace.

Throughout my journey of healing, I realized I wasn't alone. Many of us carry shame in different ways. What shame haunts you? Perhaps your shame is a byproduct of someone else's actions, their words, or behaviors. Whether intentional or not, they wounded and belittled you. Maybe someone made you feel small, unworthy, or broken beyond repair. Perhaps you were mistreated, manipulated, or abandoned and now carry shame for a story that was never yours to live.

Or are there mistakes that continue to resurface and refuse to stay in the past? Perhaps you bear the weight and guilt of an affair or an unethical business decision. Or maybe you cringe remembering a comment you made that hurt a friend, a feeling of envy or jealousy, or a lie you told to save face. Maybe your heart pounds every time you think of a stupid evening with too much alcohol, a disagreement that escalated into words and behavior that can't be taken back, or a hidden addiction that threatens your livelihood.

Shame comes in all shapes and sizes, and no one is immune to it. Whatever humiliation replays in your thoughts, threatening your sense of who you are, know this: You are in a safe place. Please be gentle with yourself in this process. The road to healing starts with acknowledging the shame and accepting the grace offered to you. Whether your shame is a result of your own doing or how you've been mistreated by others, you're right where you need to be. Jesus knows every word of your story, every moment you want to boast about and every part you try to hide behind your mask. And still, He looks at you with love, not judgment, inviting you to let go of your shame and step into His grace.

For what is hidden in shame, Jesus heals in love.

For what is hidden in shame, Jesus heals in love.

On the following pages, we will explore in greater detail how the bleeding woman's story shifts when she meets Jesus. For now, sit in this moment. Recognize that shame does not have to be your final story. There is more to come.

PRAYER

Dear God,

I am weary and burdened, exhausted by the shame I've carried for far too long. I'm tired of letting it define me. I long to be free, once and for all, from its grip. You know the things I've said and done that do not honor You, the mistakes, regrets, and humiliation that echo in my mind. While You already know the depths of my heart, I confess them to You now, laying them at Your feet. (Pause and take all the time you need at this moment.)

You know the wounds that others and this life have inflicted on me. I've been drowning in the bitterness this shame has caused me. I acknowledge all of this to You now and hold it out for You to take. (Pause and take all the time you need at this moment.)

God, the shame runs deep, but I'm ready for the healing You promise. I'm ready to release this. Even as I take this step, I know You are already holding me, working to redeem my story.

In Jesus's name, amen.

Reflect & Respond

I've never shared this story of my childhood abuse publicly. Even after years of healing, putting it into words is still difficult. But I believe it's necessary. My hope is to lead by example, to encourage you to be courageous too.

My healing began the moment I invited Light into my darkness. That same Light is available to you. You may not feel ready to let go of your shame just yet. That's okay. For today, just take one step and acknowledge it. Bring it before God. Trust that He sees you, even now.

What emotions, thoughts, and memories have this chapter stirred in you? What stories of shame are crying out for redemption? To what degree do you currently trust that your story of shame can be redeemed?

How does it feel to take a look at your shame? Notice your heartbeat, your breath, your temperature, the tension in your muscles, and the pressure in your head. Take some time to journal about how your body reacts as this moment of shame runs through your thoughts. Stay curious by removing judgment, frustration, or malice. Simply observe your response.

Who told you to hold onto this shame? Is there someone in your life who's made you feel you can't let it go? Has there been a circumstance in your life that caused you to hold tight? Again, take time to explore the root of this as you journal.

What does it feel like to imagine Jesus looking at you with

love instead of judgment? Just take one step and acknowledge it. Bring it before God. Trust that He sees you.

As our journey continues on the following pages, you'll see your shame is no match for the relentless, unbreakable love and bountiful grace of Jesus. His love sweeps away every ounce of regret with a grace that never runs dry. His mercy crushes the weight of your past mistakes, and His love is greater than all the wounds inflicted by this life.

Keep going, friend. Healing awaits.

Chapter Five

Not Just a Body

Imagine for a moment I offered you a magic wand that has the power to change your appearance. Maybe you've always wished to be taller, shorter, thinner, or fitter. Perhaps you'd use it to smooth wrinkles, erase stretch marks, or change your hair, skin, or eye color. Just a little nip here or a tuck there? I'm willing to bet nearly everyone would take advantage of this wand and wield it to fix, adjust, clear up, or simply beautify at least one body part that feels undesirable.

How do I know? Because body image struggles are everywhere in our culture. According to the National Organization for Women, by the age of 13, more than half of girls report being unhappy with their bodies. By age 17, that number jumps to 78 percent.[1] We are constantly bombarded

---

1 National Organization for Women, "Get the Facts," n.d., https://now.org/now-foundation/love-your-body/love-your-body-whats-it-all-about/get-the-facts/.

with messages that tell us we need to look a certain way to be accepted, valued, or loved. Social media, the beauty industry, and entertainment fuel this insecurity, presenting us with impossible standards that only a fraction of people naturally meet. The result? A culture that is obsessed with appearance, fueling self-doubt, comparison, and dissatisfaction.

> We are constantly bombarded with messages that tell us we need to look a certain way to be accepted, valued, or loved.

Now, let's shift our focus to someone who knew what it was like to struggle with her body, the woman in our story afflicted with a bleeding disorder. The medical condition she dealt with affected her more than just physically. Just as our culture makes body-confidence difficult, her culture played a significant role too. Her ailment made her an outcast. She was considered unclean, forced to live on the margins, isolated from community and worship. Her body had become her enemy, leaving her exhausted, rejected, and desperate. Imagine for a moment what her self-talk consisted of.

I am foul.
I am damaged. I am dirty.
I hate my body. I hate myself.

It's hard to feel beautiful in a body that feels broken.

For many women, the struggle with their body goes beyond appearance. What about the woman, like the one in our story, who feels her body has betrayed her? What about the one whose strength has been stolen by illness, whose movement has been limited by an accident, whose energy has been drained by a chronic issue? Maybe you know this struggle all too well. Maybe you've looked at your reflection and grieved what once was, what your body used to be able to do and feel, and what it allowed you to experience.

Body insecurities don't just affect how we see ourselves; they shape how we think, feel, and live. They negatively impact our identities. When we focus on what we lack, we spiral into dissatisfaction, anxiety, and even despair. Hope and courage are discovered by changing our thought patterns and allowing God to renew our mindsets.

How do we do this?

Speak to yourself with kindness. If you wouldn't say it to your best friend, don't say it to yourself. When you start tearing yourself down, replace those words with truth: "I am fearfully and wonderfully made" (Ps. 139:14 NIV).

Practice gratitude for your body. Instead of focusing on what you don't like, choose to celebrate what your body can do.

I'm grateful for these hands that create.
I'm grateful for these legs that carry me through life.
I'm grateful for these arms that embrace those I love.

Pay attention to what influences your thoughts. What you consume through social media, entertainment, or even conversations has power. If what you're taking in is feeding insecurity, it's time to filter the noise. Choose to surround yourself with encouragement and intentionally fill your heart and mind with the life-giving truth of God's Word.

Once we shift our mindset, we can treat our bodies with the love and respect they deserve. That doesn't mean striving for a certain look. It means caring for ourselves with the understanding that our bodies are gifts.

Exercise because you love your body, not because you hate it. Movement is a celebration of what your body can do, not a punishment for what you ate.

Eat well to nourish your body, not to fit an unrealistic standard. Food is fuel, not a measure of worth.

Rest because your body needs it. We are not machines. Sabbath and self-care are holy acts of trust in God's provision.

When we recognize our bodies as the only ones we'll ever get, we can treat them with the respect and care they deserve.

Furthermore, body image isn't just a mental or emotional struggle; it's a spiritual one too. When we're consumed by insecurity or fixated on our flaws and ailments, our attention drifts from our purpose. If we're too busy criticizing ourselves, we're not free to love, serve, or fully live out God's calling.

God never intended for us to live this way. He made us in His image (Gen. 1:27). He formed us with care and intention (Ps. 139:13). And He reminds us that our bodies are temples of the Holy Spirit (1 Cor. 6:19–20). This is not just a metaphor; it's a profound spiritual truth.

In the Old Testament, the temple was the sacred dwelling

place of God's presence, carefully constructed and set apart for worship (1 Kings 8:10–11). It was where God's glory rested, and because of its holiness, it was treated with the utmost reverence. But through Christ, God's presence no longer dwells in a building; it dwells within us. Our bodies have become living temples, inhabited by the Holy Spirit. That means they are sacred, valuable, and worthy of honor, not because of how they look but because of Who dwells within them.

> God does not love you less because of what your body can or cannot do.

If you feel betrayed by your body, hear this: God does not love you less because of what your body can or cannot do. You are no less whole in His eyes. Your body is not a mistake, a burden, or a failure. It is still His temple, still a vessel of His Spirit. Even in weakness, even in illness, even when it feels like your body is fighting against you, you are not less than. Scripture tells us His "power is made perfect in weakness" (2 Cor. 12:9 NIV). Your worth has never been in your physical strength, health, or capabilities. It has always been in the One who dwells within you.

I love the perspective Jess Connolly has shared: 'Your King loves your body because He made it, in His image, for His glory. Your King loves your body, not because it's a tool to get His work done with - but it's a treasure where His Spirit is housed here on earth.' Every time you breathe, every time your heart beats, every time your body endures and recovers, those are reminders that your body is resilient. Your body is a miracle, a living, breathing testimony of God's sustaining grace.[2]

Speaking of the King, let's return to the magic wand idea. If anyone could have chosen exactly how their body would look, it was Jesus. As the Creator, He had the power to design His physical appearance any way He wanted. But what does Scripture say about Him? "There was nothing beautiful or majestic about his appearance, nothing to attract us to him" (Isa. 53:2).

Jesus could have come as the most stunning, physically impressive person the world had ever seen. Instead, He came as ordinary. Why? Because He wanted to show us that He was not just a body. His body was an instrument. He used it to touch and heal the sick, wash feet, feed the hungry, carry the cross, and ultimately, lay it down in sacrifice.

Jesus could have come as the most stunning, physically impressive person the world had ever seen. Instead, He came as ordinary.

And because of His sacrifice, we are free—free from the lies that tell us our worth is in our appearance, free from the burden of insecurity, and free to live, love, and serve with

---

2 Breaking Free From Body Shame (@breakingfreefrombodyshame). (2022, July 20). "Your King loves your body because He made it . . ." Instagram. https://www.instagram.com/p/CgPxDukJ0Tm/?utm_source=ig_web_copy_link&igsh=MWRvNjEyazd4OGtsYw==

confidence. The life and healing of the woman in our story teach us that our bodies are not curses. Even when they don't work the way we wish they would, even when they change, age, and bear the scars of life, they are still worthy of care and love.

If you find yourself tearing apart your body in the mirror, pause and imagine Jesus standing beside you, placing His scarred hands on your shoulders, and saying, "Hey, that's My creation you're criticizing. You are not just a body. You are Mine."

Today, let's choose to believe Him. Let's take every thought captive, treat our bodies with love, and embrace the truth that we are more than what we see in the mirror. Our bodies are temples, instruments, and sacred vessels of God's love and purpose.

And that, my friend, is a truth worth living.

PRAYER

Dear God,

You see my struggle. As much as I've tried to move past this, I still find myself criticizing my body. I look in the mirror and only see the flaws—the extra weight, the scars, the marks, and the wrinkles. I want to be free of this chain once and for all. I want to be grateful for the body I have and stop the exhausting barrage of comparison. Please help me. And please forgive me. Forgive me for my dissatisfaction with the gift You gave me. I want to treat my body like a dwelling place worthy of Your presence. Even when it lets me down, when pain or illness limit me, help me to view and appreciate my body through Your eyes.

In Jesus's name, amen.

Reflect & Respond

Take some time to write all the things you wish you could change about your body. Go ahead. Be as picky as you'd like. It could be from an appearance, medical, or capability standpoint.

Then invite Jesus to sit with you. Read the list aloud to Him. Begin your list with this phrase: "Jesus, here are the ways I see flaws in Your design." How does He respond? Spend time with your journal, writing the words He shares with you. How does this make you feel?

Write the following verse and a body-confident affirmation on a note card to read and recite daily.

Thank you for making me so wonderfully complex! Your workmanship is marvelous—how well I know it.

—Ps. 139:14

I love my body. It has carried me through every high and every low. Each scar tells a story of strength and survival, evidence of a life fully lived. My body is a gift from

God, and I choose to honor it with love, gratitude, care, and grace.

In 1 Corinthians 6:19–20, we hear this proclamation from Paul:

> *Don't you realize that your body is the temple of the Holy Spirit, who lives in you and was given to you by God? You do not belong to yourself, for God bought you with a high price. So you must honor God with your body.*

You are a beautiful, whole temple of the Holy Spirit. Let that truth sink in for a moment. Sit in the magnitude, shock, and significance of this truth. What thoughts and emotions does it stir in you? What is one step you can take to care for your temple with greater intention to glorify God?

Chapter Six

Deep Wounds, Deeper Hope

One of my favorite pastimes is paddleboarding off the coast of North Carolina. There's something freeing about standing on the board, the sun warming my skin as I glide across the water. One day, as I paddled away from the shore, my mind drifted with each stroke. Before I knew it, I had traveled much farther than I had intended. Turning back, I quickly realized my mistake.

On my way out, the wind and current propelled me forward easily. But the return trip was different. It was grueling and daunting. I paddled twice as hard but moved at half the speed. The resistance made me feel stranded, and more than once I had to fight against rising panic. By the time I returned to the shore, I was absolutely exhausted.

We naturally desire a life like the first part of that journey, smooth and effortless with all circumstances working in our favor—college degree, career promotions, happy marriage, 2.5 kids. But life doesn't work that way. Tragedy strikes—a diagnosis, a betrayal, a loss, another negative pregnancy test, divorce papers, overdue bills. We face suffering that drains us and leaves us fighting for every inch of progress.

This is where we first meet the woman in our story. She was exhausted, worn thin, paddling against the current of life for 12 long years. She spent everything searching for relief, only to be left weaker, more isolated, and desperate for something or someone who could offer more than temporary hope.

Can you relate? Maybe your suffering has stretched across the years, leaving you drained and wondering if healing will ever come. I know that struggle firsthand. When I was 21, I experienced a sudden, heartbreaking loss that shattered my once-comfortable life. The grief left me angry, disillusioned, and lost. I'll share more of that in a later chapter, but for now, just know that I understand the ache. I know what it feels like to live in a world where the worst-case scenario happens. If I had the privilege of sitting with you, I would grieve with you. I would like to plead with God to erase your pain. We could create a list of reasons why your plight is unfair. I would put my arm around you, share a box of tissues, and shake my head in confusion.

When we are suffering, it's so difficult to see past the heartache. Our pain becomes the lens through which we see the world and how we view God. Imagine putting on a pair of glasses smeared with a filter of suffering. How does this affect your understanding of God? Typically, it would paint three possible images of God: He is either incompetent, absent, or cruel.

Take a closer look at each of these assumptions. Let's say your suffering has occurred because God is incompetent. He dropped the ball. He was inefficient in His quality control and let this mishap slip by Him. He fell asleep at the wheel. Or perhaps God is just absent. He's too busy taking care of other, larger problems in another part of the world, and He doesn't have time to be present in your life. Or we might say He is absent from this world all together. He set the world in motion and now sits back snacking on popcorn as He watches us flounder and fend for ourselves. Or maybe He is cruel, an angry God who relishes striking His wrath on His subjects over any misstep. Your suffering is a result of His discipline or anger.

These are common conclusions, but they crumble in light of Jesus. Scripture is clear that one of Jesus's purposes was to reveal the heart and nature of His Heavenly Father. "Anyone who has seen Me has seen the Father!" (John 14:9) (see also Col. 1:15, Heb. 1:3, John 1:18). See the danger in trying to understand God through the lens of your pain? It will always give you a false image. It is foolish to try to comprehend an eternal, divine being through the lens of temporary circumstances. It will fail every time. When I am tempted to view God as incompetent, absent, or cruel, I have to try to reconcile my thoughts with the life of Jesus.

And what do we see in Jesus? Compassion. Kindness. Purpose. Love.

So how do we make sense of our trials and heartaches in light of who God is? Instead of viewing Him through the lens of our difficult circumstances, we have to turn the lens around. We must choose to try to understand our suffering through the lens of a good and loving God. It doesn't make the pain disappear, but it shifts our posture.

We must choose to try to understand our suffering through the lens of a good and loving God.

Previously, we may have shouted, "God, why is this happening?" or "How could You allow something so awful?" Our heart posture begins to soften in surrender when we flip our lens: "God, I know You are good, even when life tries to convince me otherwise. Show me how to respond. Lead me through this trial in a way that honors You."

Instead of wearing the glasses of suffering, we must put on the lens of Christ. When we make the effort to see our circumstances in the context of His greater plan, we are primed for the spiritual growth and maturity that allows us to take it a step further.

Yes, it's human nature to question God when tragedy strikes. Pain wags a finger and says, "You know, if I were God, this never would've happened." But the truth is that the more we fix our eyes on Jesus, the more we realize He is who He says He is. He is all-knowing, all-loving, and all-good all the time. He is the only One who can see how all the pieces fit together for our good (Rom. 8:28).

If we continue pulling that thread, we realize that if we were God, nothing would be any different. At first, this is an incredibly tough pill to swallow. If you're like me, I immediately want to argue that point, to push back. You mean if I were God, my loved one would have still died? If I were God, that natural disaster would have still occurred, that violent crime, that accident, the mess of the coronavirus epidemic? Wars? Poverty? Hate?

Yes, even those things.

See what I mean? It's a hard pill.

But the reality is that if I were God, I would be all-knowing, all-loving, and all-good all the time, and I would know how all the pieces fit together for good. That means today would look just as it does at this moment. This is a hard but also freeing realization.

Take a deep breath and let that wash over you for a moment. Let it take root in your heart.

We were never promised lives of ease. Scripture is clear that in this world, we will have trouble (John 16:33, James 1:2–4, Ps. 34:19). We were never guaranteed a life void of despair and suffering. But we are promised that we will never walk alone. God's presence is constant and unwavering, and when we allow it, our pain draws us into the heart of our Father.

Hope always goes deeper than the hurt.

> Hope always goes deeper than the hurt.

Charles Spurgeon expressed the gift of suffering beautifully: "I have learned to kiss the waves that throw me against the Rock of Ages."

We become deeply spiritual beings, not despite our suffering but because of it. Look at the woman in our story. Her suffering led her straight to Jesus, and in one desperate act of faith, she found the fullness of healing. Imagine if this woman never experienced the plight of her physical condition. You wouldn't be holding this book right now. There would be no story to tell and no story for connection, empathy, or transformation. There would be no story worth living. God is using her story to shape yours.

So while my human instinct is to shield you from pain, I would also be blocking what only He can do in, for, and through you. We may not understand the why of our suffering, but we can trust the Who. And the One who healed this woman still sees you. He is still near. He is still working. And thanks to the gift of Jesus, we have direct access to His peace and strength. He invites us to shift from "God, why did You let this happen?" to "God, lead me through this in a way that honors You."

PRAYER

Dear God,

I'm exhausted. I connect so deeply with the woman in our story. I, too, feel drained, paddling against the relentless current of life. My pain feels unbearable at times, and I'm honestly just so fiercely mad. Life feels cruel. Unfair. And I'm tired of being tired. I don't want bitterness to steal my last shred of joy.

So even though I'm hurting, I turn to You. I know I've wrestled with You, pushed You away in frustration. I've sometimes felt like a child giving her Father the cold shoulder. Forgive me. I don't want to see You only through the lens of my despair, but it's hard to fight against it. I need You. Please help me. When every breath feels like a battle, push air into my lungs. Give me the strength to face another day. Remind me that this struggle will not last forever.

God, I know I will continue to ask why. *But please soften my heart to seek You instead of explanations. I long for Your presence, guidance, and purpose in this pain. I don't want my suffering to be in vain. Shape me in this fire.*

Refine me. Help me honor You and become more like Jesus, even here, even now.

I pray all this for Your glory and ultimately for my joy.

In Jesus's name, amen.

Reflect & Respond

Take your time at this moment. Allow the weight of the prayer to settle into your heart and expand upon it. Write it down, speak it aloud, or find a quiet space in nature to sit and pour out your thoughts to God. What past wound or current struggle do you need to share with Him today? Let your heart be open. Tell Him exactly how this pain has affected you and shaped your view of Him.

Part of your healing lies in being raw and honest. God can handle your anger, frustration, confusion, and doubts. Resist the urge to speak a perfect or polished prayer. There's no need for the "good Christian" words. Speak from your heart. Let it all come out.

After you've expressed yourself, pause.

Then ask God to show you how He has been present in your pain, even when it's hard to see. Invite Him to soften your heart and reveal a new perspective on the suffering you've experienced. Ask Him to help you see how your pain can be used for His purposes, shaping your story in ways you might not fully understand.

Take your time in this process. Your vulnerability invites transformation, and healing begins in this honest exchange with God.

What past wounds or current struggles can you share with Him today?

What big and small wins are you grateful for, despite all that feels wrong? Look closely. Make a list. Have you considered that these gifts are evidence of God's presence in your pain?

How has He shaped you through your heartache? How are you not the same woman you were before?

What steps will you take to honor God as He leads you?

Part Three

The Reach

Now we have come to the turning point in the woman's story, the moment her desperation meets Jesus's power. After years of silence, suffering, and separation, one deliberate touch changes everything. The chapters in this part will explore her courage to step forward. It will look at her healing and the miracle that drew her out of the shadows. As her story unfolds, so will yours. God is here to meet you right where you are.

Chapter Seven

Deep Calls to Deep

Everywhere Jesus went, He drew a crowd. People were drawn to His dynamic and authoritative teachings. Some came in search of a miracle, and many showed up driven by the fear of missing out. Our story of focus is no different. Within nine verses, Luke references the large crowd four times. No wonder people were confused when Jesus suddenly stopped, turned, and asked, "Who touched Me?" His disciple Peter explained the obvious: "This whole crowd is pressing up against You."

Don't miss this. Multitudes of people were pressing against Jesus, yet they did not receive His power. They were left unchanged by His presence.

This woman touched the fringe of His robe and was forever transformed. Many pressed, and just one brushed. Many were unchanged, but one was made new.

I have experienced seasons where I am one of the crowd. It's an easy drift, a slow fade. Outwardly, I'm doing all the "right" things. I'm attending church services, reading Scripture, tithing, and volunteering. Yet my faith feels dry, and God feels distant. I'm just going through the motions. I follow these practices out of habit, not out of hunger.

But this woman shows us a different way. Her act is deliberate and intentional. Her faith is personal. It is not borrowed, circumstantial, or dependent on what others are doing around her. Despite her suffering and shame, she refuses to stay on the side of the road. She allows herself to be drawn in, focused and determined. Her behavior is dangerous. She risks everything—more social disgrace, rejection, even punishment—to get to Him. She pushes through the crowd, the very source of her pain and a reminder of her disgrace, in order to get to Jesus.

Being in the vicinity of faith is not the same as having a living, authentic relationship with Jesus. This distinction is crucial, and we are forced to wrestle with this question: Are we living in casual proximity to Jesus, or are we reaching for Him with desperation?

Are we living in casual proximity to Jesus, or are we reaching for Him with desperation?

This question matters. A recent study by John Mark Comer found that while around 65 percent of Americans identify as Christian, only about 4 percent are actively following Jesus.[3] That means many are in the crowd, but few are reaching for Him. This is not what Jesus died for. The weight of this truth breaks my heart. I don't want to be someone who merely identifies as a Christian. There's too much at stake. I want to live a deliberate life where people look at me and can tell I'm His follower. The world isn't changed by apathetic Christians going through the motions. It's changed by those who've been set ablaze by His grace and can't help but share it with others.

King David, one of the most well-known figures in the Bible, was a shepherd, warrior, poet, and eventually the king of Israel. His prayers and songs, many recorded in the Psalms, reflect the raw, unfiltered emotions of someone who wrestled with life and relentlessly sought God's presence.

He was familiar with what it felt like to desperately pour out his soul for connection with God. Slowly read through his words, allowing them to connect with your own deep desire.

> *Oh God, You are my God; I earnestly search for You. My soul thirsts for You; my whole body longs for You in this parched and weary land where there is no water. I have seen You in Your sanctuary and gazed upon Your power and glory. Your unfailing love is better than life itself; how I praise You!*
>
> —Ps. 53:1–3

---

3 John Mark Comer, *Practicing the Way: Be with Jesus. Become Like Him. Do as He Did* (WaterBrook, 2024), 5.

Even in David's highest victories and lowest valleys, his story is marked by both deep devotion and devastating failure. He committed grievous sins, including abuse of power, adultery, and orchestrating a man's death. Yet he also repeatedly returned to God with a repentant heart. He was referred to as "a man after his [God's] own heart" (1 Sam. 13:14), not because he was perfect but because he continually pursued God in humility.

David's words remind us that it's okay to come to God empty, thirsty, and longing. In fact, it's in that very hunger that something sacred happens, when our deep need meets His deep love.

David also penned the phrase "Deep calls to deep" (Ps. 42:7 NIV). This verse is often interpreted as a longing for a deeper connection with God. It is one profound depth calling out to another. It's a soul's cry to move beyond surface-level faith to reach out to God with intentionality. It is arms wide open to welcome His love and transformation at a soul level.

This is the type of connection I want. It's the type of connection I want to want. I want to hunger for Jesus from the bottom of my heart. Heaven knows I don't want to just go along with the crowd and be unfazed by proximity with Him.

> I want to hunger for Jesus from the bottom of my heart.

So what does an intentional pursuit of Jesus look like? That's a personal question for each of us to explore. For me, it begins with self-awareness of my motives. Am I praying just to check a box? Or am I approaching time with Him for a vulnerable and authentic connection? Am I going to church because I feel like that's just something I'm supposed to do? Or do I walk through the doors eager for more of Him? Do I read Scripture to mark off a reading plan, or do I open His Word and anticipate divine communion?

One practice I have recently been putting into place is beginning my prayers with this: "Deep calls to deep." I take a few cleansing, deep breaths to center my heart and attention and then repeat the phrase in rhythm with my breath. I try to clear my mind and heart of any expectation other than to know Him and myself through Him. This simple practice both satisfies and fuels my hunger for Him by quieting the noise within me, and offers space for peace, clarity, and deeper awareness of His presence.

But if deep calls to deep, why is it so easy for us to linger in the shallows? We must become honestly acquainted with our deep as we seek His deep. He tenderly invites us to explore any obstacles or hesitations that threaten to keep us at a surface-level connection with Him. Imagine for a moment you are swimming in the ocean and want to explore the beauty in its depths. Now imagine your arms are full of pool noodles. Pool noodles are designed to keep you afloat. No matter how much you try to dive, they resist you. What happens when you try to drag your pool noodles down with you? They force you back to the surface.

We all have our pool noodles—barriers that keep us from drawing close to Him. Let's explore a few common ones.

- *Fear:* It wears many disguises. Maybe you're worried about what others will think if you take bold steps to follow Jesus. Or maybe you're afraid of what He might ask of you. Fear of dealing with our junk can also keep us on the surface.
- *Anger:* You've been so deeply hurt or felt abandoned by what God did or didn't allow that keeping Him at a distance feels like the only way to protect your heart. Bitterness and resentment have isolated you.
- *Insecurity:* Perhaps you don't reach out to Jesus because you don't believe you are worthy or welcome to do so.
- *Busyness:* You have a relentless drive to be productive and accomplish your to-do list. It can be especially tricky because it often disguises itself as responsibility or faithfulness. But if you're too busy doing things *for* God that you don't make space to be *with* God, that busyness becomes a barrier.
- *Misconception:* A view of an angry, unapproachable God will surely keep someone hiding at a distance among the crowd.

No matter the source of your hesitation, let the bleeding woman's story encourage you. She didn't have to beg or prove herself. She didn't have to have all the answers; she just had to reach out. In the pages that follow, we will explore Jesus's power and goodness that welcomed her touch. But in the meantime, take comfort in this verse: "Come close to God, and God will come close to you" (James 4:8).

Like the woman who reached for the hem of Jesus's garment, may we, too, reach for Him with a faith that defies logic, believing His power is greater than our limitations. You have one life. Don't spend it drifting.

Take a risk. Dive deep. Reach for Him with deliberate intention.

PRAYER

Dear God,

Thank You for opening my eyes to this crucial aspect of Your encounter with this courageous woman. Watching as her eyes are locked on You, pushing through the crowd she once avoided to reach out and touch You has inspired and convicted me. I admit there are times my faith is complacent, and I am just in the crowd, present but passive. I want a "reaching-out" kind of faith, expectant and hungry for Your presence.

Set my heart on fire for more of You and stir a hunger in me that only You can satisfy. Open my eyes to any hesitation in me that serves as an obstacle. Help me to call out the things that threaten to keep my connection with You at a shallow, surface level. Deep calls to deep, and I feel You drawing me closer. I don't want to stay in the shallows. Today, I answer that call—fully, completely, and with my whole heart.

In Jesus's name, amen.

Reflect & Respond

Breath Prayer: This powerful, centering practice helps quiet your mind and attune your heart to God's presence. Find a quiet space and set a timer for five to ten minutes. Sit comfortably, close your eyes, and breathe slowly and deeply.

With each inhale, silently pray, "Deep calls . . ."

With each exhale, silently pray, ". . . to deep."

Let this become your sacred rhythm, your soul's quiet response to God's invitation. With each breath, you move from distraction into devotion, from surface-level routine into soulful connection. Allow the repetition to settle your spirit and deepen your awareness of God's nearness.

Reach Prayer: This prayer practice uses a simple physical motion—reaching your hand—to guide your heart into a deeper connection with Jesus. Slowly extend your hand in front of you, palm open, as if reaching for the hem of His garment. Picture Jesus in front of you, attentive and present.

Now look at each of your five fingers. Let each one represent a specific longing. For example:

Thumb: Peace
Pointer finger: Wisdom for something ahead
Middle finger: Courage to face a fear
Ring finger: Healing in a relationship
Pinky finger: Hope or a personal need

Alternatively, you can assign a name to each finger—the people you are praying for—placing them figuratively in the hand you're lifting to Jesus.

As you move finger by finger, speak their name or need out loud or in your heart, symbolically handing each one over to Him.

When you pray with an open hand instead of a clenched fist, it becomes a posture of surrender and trust. It symbolizes your willingness to release what you cannot control and your readiness to receive the blessings God longs to place in your hand.

This prayer is simple and profound. It anchors your body and soul in the posture of faith, the kind that reaches. Like the woman in Luke 8, you're not pressing aimlessly through a crowd. You are reaching on purpose.

Reflect & Respond

In what areas of your faith are you just going through the motions or checking boxes?

What are your "pool noodles?" Review the list shared in this chapter. What in you hesitates to deliberately reach out to Jesus?

What small step can you take to be more intentional in your relationship with Jesus?

Chapter Eight

The Power of the Touch

A small, clay figurine sits on my desk. It was crafted by the hands of our son Jacob when he was around five years old. It's his representation of his dad—my husband, Chad. "Clay Chad" is about 6 inches tall and what you would expect small, amateur hands to create. He has little T-rex looking arms that protrude from his sides. One ear is missing, and one foot is square while the other is round. A toothpick was used to carve out a crude nose, two eyes, and a mouth. In short, it looks nothing like my husband. The gap between this small figurine and the reality it aims to represent is too staggering for words.

In the same way, our attempts to grasp the essence of God fall short. There is a massive gap between the image of God in our minds and the reality of who He is. His sheer grandeur is no match for our limited understanding. Our efforts to shrink God into something manageable are feeble, like trying to mold the infinite with a child's lump of clay. He is beyond our comprehension, vast and uncontainable. This in and of itself is not a negative thing. It's human nature. However, we must maintain an awareness that the gap will exist until we meet Him face to face. It's how we view and address the gap that matters.

I remember the day Jacob presented Clay Chad as a gift to his dad. It was Father's Day, and Jacob was bursting with pride to give him his present. When Chad opened the work of art, his face was illuminated with a smile, and he gave our son a huge hug. He gushed with admiration as he pointed out the vibrant paint colors and the obvious care and time Jacob took to create it. Chad was so honored to have received such a thoughtful gift from his son.

Notice what he *didn't* say. He didn't say, "What's wrong with you? Can't you see this looks nothing like me? You really fell short in your poor effort." Of course not! Chad knew it didn't matter that the finished product wasn't an accurate depiction of reality. He was focused on our son's heartfelt intention behind his work.

I keep this little figurine on my desk as a representation of how I fall short of fully grasping the truest version of my Heavenly Father. It's my visual reminder that He is better and bigger than we can grasp. Our limited understanding of God doesn't diminish His love for us. Just as Chad was genuinely thrilled by his son's gift, our Father is thrilled each time we come to Him. He delights in our efforts to connect and get to know Him better. He doesn't want our perfection;

He wants our curiosity and openness. And isn't that a wonderful, freeing truth?

That gives me perspective, not just on God but also on how we relate to Him over time. Imagine my little son's glee when he presented his dad with this gift he'd put such time and attention into. He was proud, confident, and unencumbered. The possibility that his gift was anything less than excellent didn't even cross his mind. Jacob is now a young adult. Imagine if he were to create a clay model of his dad today. He would be hypercritical of his work, frustrated, and embarrassed, overtly aware of his lack of artistic ability. He probably wouldn't smile or even look his dad in the eye as he passed the finished product over as an offering. His energy level would starkly contrast that of his childhood self. That shift mirrors what can happen in our spiritual lives. As adults, we often trade childlike confidence for self-consciousness and fear of falling short.

Jesus once encouraged His followers to "'become like little children'" (Matt. 18:3). He emphasized the importance of humility, trust, and dependence on God, qualities children naturally possess. God delights in our sincere, unfiltered faith and curiosity rather than our perfection.

God delights in our sincere, unfiltered faith and curiosity rather than our perfection.

Our childlike faith is not about ignorance but about trust. It's about believing that even when we don't fully understand God, He is still good, still powerful, and still near. The woman who reached for the hem of Jesus's robe did not stop to analyze every theological implication. She allowed herself to draw closer.

The story of the woman offers more than a moment of miraculous healing; it reveals layers of cultural and spiritual significance. Take a moment to explore an often overlooked cultural aspect of this story. Luke was sure to point out that the woman reached out and touched the fringe, or hem, of Jesus's robe. Jesus was likely wearing a tzitzit, tassels Jewish men were commanded to wear (Num. 15:37–41, Deut. 22:12). These tassels symbolized God's commandments and His authority and were worn as a physical reminder to live according to His ways.

Furthermore, many believed the Messiah would "rise with healing in his wings" (Mal. 4:2), and some rabbis interpreted "wings" as referring to the corners of a garment. The symbolism gives us an even greater appreciation of this story. So perhaps the woman wasn't just reaching for a random part of Jesus's robe. Maybe she was reaching for an item symbolizing divine authority and obedience to God. Could her touch indicate her faith in His divine nature?

In Jewish tradition, ritual purity was paramount. To be unclean meant being socially and religiously cut off. But Jesus wasn't just a rabbi. He was the fulfillment of the Law itself. Instead of being contaminated by her touch, His holiness overpowered her impurity, restoring her completely. Remember that according to Mosaic Law, if an unclean person touched someone else, that person was also unclean until evening and had to bathe in a cleansing ceremony and launder his clothing. But these laws didn't bind Jesus. His response didn't just defy expectations; it revealed His divine nature. He came to fulfill the Law and make things new. He came to change the system that was confining. He came to reveal the heart of God the Father, including His love, grace, and mercy for His people. Jesus was a reflection of the Father, divine in authority and full of grace, in a world governed by an increasingly impossible set of 613 religious laws. He set forth the law of love to replace condemnation and shame.

Jesus's majesty is on display and must not be overlooked. Consider the mechanics of a heart valve. It ensures that blood flows in only one direction by preventing backflow, keeping the heart functioning as it was designed. During Jesus's encounter with this woman, His healing power flowed out of Him, but her uncleanliness did not flow into Him. He was immune to what caused society to shun and isolate her. This is the beauty of Jesus. His purity is not fragile. His holiness doesn't flinch at our mess. Instead, His power flows only one way, to bring restoration, healing, and transformation. This is the very nature of our Savior, divine authority wrapped in perfect love. It's a truth that should make our hearts expand with deep gratitude. The power of His divinity and the compassion of His humanity are on full display.

We may be incapable of fully grasping His greatness, just like my son's figurine was insufficient at capturing his father's likeness. But our Father does not demand perfect understanding. He invites us to trust Him anyway. May the Jesus we meet in this story deepen our awe and widen our trust, reminding us that while the gap between our understanding and God is vast, His love always bridges it.

PRAYER

Dear God,

Wow! Reflecting on this encounter is expanding my understanding of just how wonderful You are. Forgive me for the times I've limited You, for trying to put You in a box. Thank You for Your grace, which is always there when I fall short of fully understanding Your goodness, power, compassion, and sovereignty.

I'm so grateful for the accounts of Jesus's life, knowing You gave us His story so we can see Your true nature and goodness on display. Please continue to open my eyes to Your limitless love. I am honored and humbled to be on this journey with You, and my heart is eager to know You more.

In Jesus's name, amen.

Reflect & Respond

Where have you unintentionally shaped God into something manageable (like the clay figurine) rather than embracing

His mystery and majesty? Reflect on moments when you've tried to understand or control God. What would it look like to release that need and trust?

Suggestion: Grab Play-Doh or modeling clay and sculpt something meaningful to you—a person, a cross, or a symbol of God's presence in your life. Let it reinforce the idea that your best representations of God are still limited. As you shape the clay, reflect on how you've tried to "shape" God in your mind and how much greater He actually is.

In what areas of your life have you underestimated Jesus's power to heal, restore, or transform? The woman didn't just touch His robe; she reached for His divine authority. What have you been hesitant to bring to Him, perhaps believing it's too messy or broken?

Invitation to Respond: Close your eyes and picture yourself reaching for the hem of Jesus's garment. What are you hoping to receive? What are you trusting Him with in this moment? Write it down, speak it aloud, or sit silently and let the image settle in your heart.

Suggestion: Cut some ribbon or string to tie together as a tassel, a modern tzitzit, to symbolize that God's presence, promises, and power are within reach. Hold it during prayer, and let it remind you that Jesus is both fully divine and deeply personal.

Chapter Nine

Called Out

It happened in an instant. One moment, I was soaking up a carefree summer weekend at the beach with my husband, two sons, and some close friends. The next moment, panic surged through me. I couldn't find Ben, our youngest son. He was only two and a half, not a strong swimmer, and he wasn't wearing his life jacket. My eyes frantically scanned the water. My heart pounded as I hurried along the shore, calling his name. Then I saw him. He was safe, playing with a friend behind one of the boats. Relief washed over me, but something else lingered.

A thought flashed through my mind in that moment of panic that was so instinctual and raw that it shocked me: "Oh, so it's going to be Ben."

I wasn't just afraid something had happened to him. I was *expecting* it. That realization unsettled me. Why would I expect a traumatic loss? Why was my first response not just fear but grief? I didn't have the full answer yet, but something in me knew this was bigger than a single moment of panic.

Looking back, I can see where it began. I was 21, a senior in college, and had just spent a weekend at home with my mom for a family reunion. She was a 5'2" ball of energy, lighting every room and making everyone feel seen and valued. Just days later, she mentioned pain in her neck. She saw an orthopedist who diagnosed her with bursitis and sent her home with a neck brace. All the while, she was having a massive heart attack that would take her life.

Mom was my rock, my biggest cheerleader, and the steady heartbeat of my world. Our relationship was full of love, deep conversations, and a connection that felt unbreakable. But in an instant, she was gone.

The cruelest irony? Just days before she died, Mom and I had been on the phone celebrating my completion of a 14-page paper for my psychology class on the topic of parental loss. I had just spent weeks studying the grief process, researching family dynamics, and analyzing how people cope with death.

So when it happened to me, my Type-A overachieving personality kicked in. I thought I was prepared. Grief became another challenge to master, another task to complete. I believed I could do grief "right," as if there were a grade attached.

I was kidding myself. Nothing could have prepared me for the sheer force of grief. The pain was stunning, severe, and consuming. There were days I felt like I couldn't breathe.

I moved through life in a fog, performing normal tasks but always aware of the gaping hole in my world.

Nothing could have prepared me for the sheer force of grief.

And while life moved on, the grief remained. It lingered beneath the surface of my adult life in subtle ways I didn't fully recognize until that day at the beach. Sitting with my emotions that day, I understood what God was showing me. I spent years living in a quiet state of anticipatory grief, waiting for loss to strike again. Without realizing it, I had built a wall around my heart, believing that if I could brace myself, maybe, just maybe, the pain wouldn't be as devastating the next time.

However, that wall didn't just protect me from pain. It kept me from love. It dulled the joy of connection. It held my husband and my boys at arm's length. The constant state of bracing for impact had isolated me.

On the drive home, tears streamed as I turned to Chad and voiced my realization. I didn't want to live this way anymore. I wanted to be fully present with my family, not half-hidden behind a shield of fear. I wanted to love freely without the shadow of impending loss hanging over me.

It wasn't until that moment that I understood I had been hiding—hiding from pain, yes, but also hiding from love. The walls I built were sturdy, crafted over years from fear, grief, and self-protection. They felt safe, like a fortress. But they were also a prison. I thought I was protecting myself, but in reality, I was missing out on the fullness of life God had for me. That day, I knew I could no longer stay hidden.

> I thought I was protecting myself, but in reality, I was missing out on the fullness of life God had for me.

I share this because as I reflected on the bleeding woman's encounter with Jesus, I realized her story wasn't so different from mine. She knew she "could not stay hidden" (Luke 8:47). She had spent years suffering, unseen, withdrawing into the shadows. But Jesus didn't let her stay there.

Jesus stopped. He turned and asked, "Who touched Me?" But of course, He already knew. As the crowd looked around in confusion, He locked eyes with her, this beautiful woman who had been invisible to the world for so long. For the first time in years, someone had acknowledged her with love, not rejection. Jesus's expression beckoned her safely out of the shadows. He called her out.

And this moment wasn't just for her. It's for us too.

Pause a moment to imagine yourself in a similar scene. Picture Jesus in front of you, giving you the same nonverbal cues. Allow the distractions of your surroundings to fade as your eyes are drawn in and entirely focused on Jesus. Look at His loving, tender, compassionate expression solely for you. Breathe in His peace and exhale any fear. Spend as much time as you need here, asking Jesus to reveal truths to you as He lovingly calls you out. Let Him guide you as you consider what you might be hiding behind and what you might be hiding from.

We often hide behind things that give us a sense of control or safety such as busyness, perfection, or success. Perhaps you've found comfort in staying active, assuming that if you keep moving you can outrun the fear or pain that lingers just beneath the surface. Are you afraid that stepping off the hamster wheel of productivity will leave you in a stillness so quiet that it demands you hear His voice and face truths you've been avoiding?

Or maybe you're hiding behind a mask of normalcy. You've built a life that appears put together, thinking that if you present yourself in a certain way, others won't see your weaknesses or struggles. A carefully curated image of perfection makes a strong wall to hide behind.

Success, too, can become a shield, a way to prove your worth and distract from the deeper vulnerabilities that lie within. Or perhaps it's insecurity that has kept your comfort zone small, convincing you it's safer not to try. You might be hiding behind excuses, bad habits, or fears.

And what are you hiding *from*? Is it the deeper connections and intimacy that might make you feel too exposed, too vulnerable? Are you hiding from a higher calling or purpose that feels too daunting or uncertain?

Perhaps like so many of us, you are hiding from forgiveness, either offering it to someone else or accepting it for yourself. Are you hiding from exposure, telling yourself you have that addiction or tendency under control? Or is it possible you're hiding from a call to serve, to help a neighbor, or to show up in your community in a way that stretches you?

Walls come in so many shapes and sizes. Constructing protective barriers around our hearts and minds is human nature. These walls form a comfortable place to live and often a necessary space to heal from mistreatment or pain. But over time, the walls we hide behind keep us in one place and prevent us from living the life God has planned for us.

Hiding might make us feel safe, but it actually keeps us stuck. Growth and peace come when we recognize and name our walls.

Jesus is calling you out. Sometimes when we think of being called out, we may fear disapproval or judgment as if we've done something wrong. But that's not how Jesus calls us. He isn't wagging His finger at you in condemnation. He isn't calling you out to shame you; He's calling you forward to heal you. Jesus calls us into the light to expose our flaws, not to condemn us, but to bring us joy and illuminate His glory.

He isn't calling you out to shame you; He's calling you forward to heal you.

Consider Ephesians 2:10: "For we are God's masterpiece. He has created us anew in Christ Jesus, so we can do the good things he planned for us long ago."

Masterpieces weren't carefully and intentionally crafted to be hidden away in a dark room. What a travesty that would be! Instead, masterpieces are destined to be on display with a spotlight illuminating their beauty and purpose to display the great work of their creator.

First Peter 2:9 (NIV) reminds us, "But you are a chosen people, a royal priesthood, a holy nation, God's special possession, that you may declare the praises of him who called you out of darkness into his wonderful light."

God didn't create you and give you one life just to hide. Jesus didn't die on the cross for you to remain hidden behind the false security of walls.

The woman from our story understood this in an instant, and she chose to be courageous. She knew she had to step forward, even before she knew what Jesus would say or do in response. Jesus didn't force her. He only set the scene and waited patiently for her realization that she could no longer stay hidden.

And just like the woman in the crowd, we don't realize how much we're missing until we answer Jesus's call. Are you ready to answer Him and step out of the shadows in faith?

The first step begins with naming your walls. You will know you've identified them because a deep, visceral reaction will stir in you when you see them and recognize all they're robbing of you. It's time to be righteously indignant. It's time to pull out a sledgehammer and let the demolition begin. No one is going to do this for you. Start swinging with all your resolve because on the other side of these walls stands the woman God created you to be. She's the one who is unashamed and free to love, lead, and live out her God-given purpose. And she's waiting for you to meet her.

PRAYER

Dear God,

Please give me Your strength and wisdom. Reveal to me what I've been hiding behind and from. I'm listening. (Be still. Pause here as long as you need.)

I see it now. All the ways I've made myself small. I've allowed fears, doubts, past pain, and excuses to build walls that have shrunk my comfort zone.

And yes, now I'm outraged. I may not have asked for or created the circumstances that built the foundation for my walls, but I'm the one who chose to remain behind them. No longer! You've given me one life. I don't want to be telling the same story of excuses five years from now. The next step of my transformation begins now. I hear You calling me out of the shadows, and today I am answering "Yes!"

Give me endurance and perseverance to keep swinging until every square inch of my walls are down once and for all. Thank You for loving me too much to keep me hidden.

I love You. And I'm so excited for the freedom and transformation ahead!

In Jesus's name, amen.

Reflect & Respond

What are you hiding behind? What current excuses have been keeping you stagnant? Make a list in your journal.

Who told you that you had to hide? Is there a person or life circumstance that told you to build your walls?

What are you hiding from? Pause to consider this question and journal your thoughts. Think big. This is your chance to explore what you've been avoiding.

What is your hiding costing you? How would your life change if you stopped hiding?

Imagine taking a sledgehammer to your walls and exerting all your energy and effort to get the job done. How does that feel?

Chapter Ten

At His Feet

The woman who reached out for Jesus has been called out, and now we witness her powerful, vivid response. Luke paints the scene. Her reaction is so consuming that her body visibly trembles. At first glance, we might assume she's shaking from fear. After all, she had been conditioned to expect rejection, to anticipate shame. For 12 years she had been treated with disdain and dismissed as unclean. Remember, according to Mosaic Law, her touch should have defiled this man. To the watching crowd, it may have looked like she collapsed at His feet to beg for forgiveness and plead for absolution.

However, Luke includes a key detail that refutes this assumption. *She knew she had been immediately healed* (Luke 8:44). It is more likely that her trembling was not from fear but from overwhelming awe and gratitude. The magnitude of what had just happened and the realization that her deepest longing had suddenly become a reality was too much to contain. The weight of the moment and the flood of emotion left her unable to stand.

In a single moment, she realized Jesus was the One in whom all hope is found.

And yet there's another layer. She wasn't just trembling because of what happened to her. She was trembling because of Who was standing before her. In a single moment, she realized Jesus was the One in whom all hope is found.

To fully grasp the weight of her posture, let's review the spiritual and cultural system that shaped her reality. Consider the design of the Jerusalem temple. The outermost area was called the Court of Women—as close as women were permitted to enter. The innermost sanctuary, the Holy of Holies, was where the presence of God dwelled. Women were allowed to observe sacred ceremonies outside the Holy of Holies from a balcony above the court. And due to her condition, this woman wasn't even allowed near the temple at all.

Now we understand her reaction more fully. For years, she had sought healing, not only to be free from her affliction but also to be welcomed back into the Court of Women and counted among those who could approach the dwelling place of God.

But now she wasn't just near the temple; she was face to face with God Himself. Jesus referred to His own body as the true temple (John 2:19–21). The woman who had been prohibited from the temple had just reached out and touched the Temple Himself. And so of course she fell to her knees, not in shame, not in fear, but in absolute reverence and heartfelt worship.

Interestingly, she was not alone in this posture. Rewind our story a bit, and we see she wasn't the first person to bend a knee in front of Jesus. Jairus was a synagogue leader, a highly respected and influential figure in his community (Luke 8:41, Mark 5:22). His position meant he was responsible for the administration of the synagogue, organizing worship services, and ensuring the proper teaching of the Law. Because of this, he would have been closely associated with the religious elite, many of whom were skeptical of or outright opposed to Jesus.

It was unusual for a man of Jairus's status to fall to his knees before Jesus. Bowing before another person was an act of humility and desperation that would have risked his reputation and position. Jewish men, particularly those in leadership, were not expected to show outward displays of submission, especially in public. Kneeling was an act of reverence typically reserved for worshiping God. Jairus's posture aligned him with the person the religious leaders sought to discredit.

Despite these obstacles, Jairus's love for his dying daughter outweighed his pride and position. His actions demonstrated raw faith and utter dependence on Jesus, showing that even a man of great influence recognized Jesus as the only hope when faced with a deep need. Just like the woman from our story, Jairus had likely exhausted every earthly option such as doctors, religious rituals, and prayers, yet none had the power to save his daughter. He turned to Jesus as his only true hope, not as a last resort.

When was the last time His goodness brought me to my knees?

I picture Jairus and this beautiful woman at the feet of Jesus, and their experiences undo me. The desperation, humility, and hope on Jairus's face and the sheer joy, elation, and adoration radiating from hers are both captivating and inspiring. And I have to ask myself in response: When was the last time I trembled before Jesus? When was the last time His goodness brought me to my knees?

In an age where faith can become casual, we risk losing the awe that should accompany our encounters with Jesus. The danger lies in what author Paul David Tripp calls "awe amnesia," our tendency to forget the majesty of God as we become too familiar with Him. Tripp writes, "Awe is the fuel that drives the worship of the heart. We cannot worship what we do not marvel at. The more we marvel at something, the more we are moved to worship."[4] This awe is what makes the woman's response so powerful. She fell at Jesus's feet, not just in reverence but because her heart was gripped by the magnificence of who He is.

We need to protect ourselves from allowing familiarity

---

4 Paul David Tripp, *Awe: Why It Matters for Everything We Think, Say, & Do* (Crossway, 2015), 112.

to breed complacency. Faith isn't just something we do; it's who we are. It shapes the way we think, speak, and live. And at the heart of our faith is the recognition that Jesus is our only hope, not just for eternity but for today—for every fear, every need, and every broken place within us. When we allow ourselves to lose that sense of awe, Jesus becomes a figure we know about instead of someone we deeply know. Let this woman's encounter reignite a passion for Jesus in your own heart. He is calling you to return to a posture of holy reverence where faith is not merely intellectual but deeply experiential. He is calling you out to the deep trust that Jairus and this woman displayed, the trust that He alone is enough.

> At the heart of our faith is the recognition that Jesus is our only hope, not just for eternity but for today–for every fear, every need, and every broken place within us.

Developing intentional rhythms can help us answer the call to a posture of reverence before Jesus. When we build practices that bring us into His presence, partnering with the Holy Spirit, we can fuel and sustain our sense of awe. In addition to the journaling practice you're engaging in through our journey together, here are a few other suggestions.

- *Intentional Prayer:* Set aside time each day to engage in heartfelt prayer. Use it as a chance to be in His presence and acknowledge His greatness, not just to share requests. In those moments, allow the magnitude of God's love and power to captivate you.

- *Stillness:* In our busy world, finding moments of stillness is vital. Quiet your mind, free from distractions, and sit in the peace of His presence. Being still before God allows us to experience His holiness and feel awe in the quiet.
- *Worship Music:* Music has a powerful way of stirring our hearts toward reverence. Surround yourself with worship music that reminds you of who God is—His greatness, majesty, and goodness. Allow the lyrics to stir your heart into worship.

You can rekindle your awe and reverence for Jesus by intentionally integrating rhythms into your life. Let them become consistent ways to answer the call to worship Him wholeheartedly.

I can relate to Jairus. There have been moments in my life when fear and overwhelming need have driven me to my knees. Each time, my tear-streaked face presses to the floor as I plead for God's intervention in a difficult circumstance. My cries are raw and unfiltered, a desperate acknowledgment that He is my only hope. And while I wouldn't choose the trials that bring me to this place, I am profoundly grateful for what they produce in me—a deeper realization that Jesus alone is my refuge. Even in the midst of my begging and pleading, I find myself surrendering, ending my prayer with a cry to trust Him more, no matter how He chooses to move.

I can also relate to this woman. There have been countless moments when I've stood on the other side of an answered prayer, overwhelmed as gratitude, relief, and unfiltered awe bring me to my knees. Each time, I am struck by the graciousness of God, by the brilliance of His light piercing through the darkness that once felt insurmountable. I know what it is to be completely undone by His faithfulness.

One of my most defining falling-to-my-knees moments was when my husband, Chad, began experiencing odd vision symptoms. He described seeing waves and distortions in straight lines such as power lines, window blinds, and the edges of walls. An appointment with his ophthalmologist led to a referral to a retina specialist, and within a week, his condition worsened rapidly. The hours-long specialist appointment brought the diagnosis: macular telangiectasia (MacTel).

The doctor asked Chad if he had diabetes (no) and if he snored (yes). He explained how both could contribute to MacTel, but if diabetes wasn't the cause, he had seen cases where snoring causes a lack of oxygen that produces mini aneurysms in the retina, causing them to bleed and distort vision. The doctor was confident that treating his sleep apnea with a continuous positive airway pressure machine (CPAP) would help stop the damage and potentially restore his sight.

We left the appointment in a daze, and like so many do in moments of uncertainty, we turned to Google. Dread creeped in as every piece of research we found stated there was no cure, and vision loss was inevitable. Chad could not read his phone or computer screen by this point due to the rapid progression. While the doctor's words gave us a sliver of hope, the bleak research and Chad's accelerating symptoms filled us with uncertainty.

The what-ifs gripped me with fear. I wrestled with the thought of my strong, independent husband losing his sight. He runs a company and loves to travel, cook, fish, and hunt. How would this change our lives? Would he ever see the faces of our future grandchildren? What if he could never again do the things that bring him joy? How would we cope?

In this season of waiting and unknowns, I found myself, like Jairus, brought to my knees, crying out to the Lord for healing for someone I love. When the what-ifs put me in a spiral, I had friends and family remind me to focus on the even-ifs. My ultimate hope was not in a medical opinion or treatment plan. Whether in healing or hardship, I knew Jesus would sustain us. My anchor in this storm was Jesus. I found comfort in clinging to the promise that He is still good, *even if* our lives look different than we imagined. *Even if* Chad were to lose his vision, we had to trust that joy and purpose would still be possible.

After eight weeks of consistently using the CPAP machine, Chad returned for a follow-up scan. The results confirmed what we had dared to hope. His vision was improving; the damage was reversing. Relief and gratitude flooded us, emotions so overwhelming that I later found myself again on my knees, much like the woman in Scripture, this time in sheer worship. I poured out my praise, not only for the healing but for what the journey had revealed. I had taken so much for granted. This experience gave me a fresh perspective on what truly matters.

Even now, I catch glimpses of Chad chopping vegetables, baiting a hook, or reading a book, and my heart swells with gratitude. Quietly I offer a prayer of thanksgiving, not just for his restored vision but for a deeper trust in the One who holds all things together.

I don't know what has brought you to your knees. Confession? Repentance? Gratitude? Perhaps desperation? But I do know every time you bow before Him, it is an act of worship. So bend a knee.

Your heavenly Father is already there, waiting to meet you with His unfailing love and assurance.

PRAYER

Dear God,

You have called me out, and now I ask you to wake me up. Awaken me to Your majesty and presence. You are the King of kings and the Lord of lords, and yet I so easily take it for granted that You want a relationship with me. Your goodness and power exist all around me every day, yet I've allowed complacency to blind me.

Oh, how I envy the woman from our story! I see the intimate connection with You as she unabashedly quakes and falls to her knees in front of You. I want that too. Forgive my complacency. You are worthy of my praise, attention, and worship. Deep calls to deep, and I long for awe to become part of my regular practice with You. Guide me, and I will follow.

In Jesus's name, amen.

Reflect & Respond

Consider aspects other than God that capture your awe. Is it material possessions, other people, accomplishments, or even yourself? What does this realization stir in you?

When was the last time you trembled before God? What was the circumstance? What specifically elicited such a reaction? If you don't recall such an experience, journal how this makes you feel. What has prevented such an experience for you?

Spend a few moments on your knees, just like our woman. Lay your journal on the floor in front of you and write phrases about God's goodness. Make a list of the things you're grateful for. Pray over your list and thank Jesus for all He is to you. Ask Him to continue to open your heart to His goodness and your eyes to His gifts all around you.

Chapter Eleven

Where's My Miracle?

Some read the story of this woman's miraculous healing and feel the sting of disappointment rise in their chest. Maybe you're one of them. You are tempted to shut your Bible and turn away because this story hits a wound that's still raw. You've prayed, you've believed, you've held on. So why does it feel like heaven is silent? Maybe you want to scream, "I have been reaching out and touching Your cloak too. Where is *my* miracle?"

Maybe you want to scream, "I have been reaching out and touching Your cloak too. Where is *my* miracle?"

I see you. I am so sorry for the life circumstances that have left you dismayed. Your heartache is real. Your waiting is not unnoticed. Your pain is safe here. You don't have to rush past your disappointment. You don't have to pretend it doesn't hurt. This chapter is for you.

Many of us are praying for a miracle right now, pleading for a medical cure, restoration in a broken relationship, freedom from addiction, or any other gift that feels just out of reach. I know how heavy that waiting can feel. I've been praying for God's intervention in a situation for years. I understand what it's like to sound like a broken record in prayer, repeating the same request. When nothing seems to change, it's easy to wonder if God is listening.

> You don't have to pretend it doesn't hurt.

As we explored in Chapter Six, suffering can taint our view of God, making us question His presence and goodness. Trials can also make us feel like we're doing something wrong and that we aren't good enough Christians, so it's no wonder we wrestle with discouragement and doubt. Maybe I didn't pray hard enough. Maybe my faith isn't strong enough.

Maybe God is just silent.

But faith is not a currency we exchange for miracles. Otherwise, we reduce God to a vending machine, dispensing blessings only when we've inserted the right amount of belief. When we approach this story that way, we miss its deeper truth.

When Mary, the mother of Jesus, became pregnant, she went to visit her cousin Elizabeth. Their conversation, filled with joy and wonder, offers a new perspective on blessing that is poignant to our topic. Elizabeth, in her excitement over Mary's pregnancy, proclaimed, "You are blessed because you believed that the Lord would do what he said" (Luke 1:45).

At first glance, this seems to mean that belief produces a blessing or that faith leads to a miracle. But what if Elizabeth was saying something even deeper?

What if belief itself is the blessing?

Maybe it's not an either/or but a both/and. Belief can lead to a blessing, *and* belief is a blessing. This shifts the focus. It suggests that being blessed isn't just about receiving what we long for but how our hearts respond in faith to God's presence.

If I believe Elizabeth's words, that the Lord will do what He said, then perhaps that trust is a blessing just as much as, if not more than, than any tangible gift or favorable circumstance He may provide. Could it be that the greatest miracle isn't in the outcome but in the transformation that happens within us as we believe?

Could it be that the greatest miracle isn't in the outcome but in the transformation that happens within us as we believe?

You've been introduced to parts of my story that I've woven throughout our journey together. So you know I've been on both sides of this. If the doctor's advice for Chad had failed, if Chad's vision had continued to decline, my hope would have remained steadfast because my confidence was never in a cure. It was in Christ. Whether in healing or hardship, I knew He would sustain us.

Even though I didn't receive the miracle I pleaded for and lost my mom too soon, I know God is still sovereign, loving, and working all things for my good. I have seen how He has used my heartache and faith to shape me more into the image of Jesus. And while I still wish I had had more time with my mom, I've seen how in loss, faith can be a miracle, one that carries us forward, even when the result we long for doesn't come.

We can find such hope in the words and life of the Apostle Paul. Let's look at a few parts of his letter to the early Christians in the city of Philippi. In Philippians 4:4, Paul wrote, "Always be full of joy in the Lord. I say it again—rejoice!" When does he encourage us to be full of joy in the Lord? *Always.* Even in our waiting, our doubt, and our uncertainty? Even in suffering? *Yes.* Always means always.

Philippians 4:6 says, "Don't worry about anything; instead, pray about everything. Tell God what you need, and thank Him for all He has done." Paul again uses the language of absolutes—anything, everything. There's no part of our lives that's too small, too messy, or too overwhelming for God. He invites us to bring it all—every worry, every request, every moment of gratitude.

This isn't just about praying in crisis; it's about cultivating a rhythm of conversation with the One who listens. Tell Him what you need. Thank Him for what He's already done.

Paul goes on to say in Philippians 4:7, "Then you will experience God's peace, which exceeds anything we can understand. His peace will guard your hearts and minds as you live in Christ Jesus." Notice what the verse *doesn't* say. Paul doesn't encourage Christ-followers to present their needs to God so He will answer all our prayers as we hope. He doesn't say you will have a life of ease. No, he promises something far greater—"God's peace, which exceeds anything we can understand." The beautiful gift of peace will protect your heart and mind as you unite with Jesus. Wow! Let that sink in.

"And now, dear brothers and sisters, one final thing. Fix your thoughts on what is true, and honorable, and right, and pure, and lovely, and admirable. Think about things that are excellent and worthy of praise" (Phil. 4:8). Paul understood the power of our mindsets and our capacity to choose the focus of our thoughts. We can allow bitterness to sink in by fixing our thoughts on all that is unfair. Or we can fix our thoughts on the evidence of God's presence and peace, no matter our circumstances.

"Not that I was ever in need, for I have learned how to be content with whatever I have. I know how to live on almost nothing or with everything. I have learned the secret of living in every situation, whether it is with a full stomach or empty, with plenty or little. For I can do everything through Christ, who gives me strength" (Phil. 4:11–13). Contentment is a state of deep satisfaction and peace, independent of external circumstances. It means finding joy and gratitude in the present moment rather than constantly striving for more or being unsettled by what is lacking. True contentment is not complacency or passivity but a heart posture of trust, especially in God's provision, timing, and goodness.

"Even so, you have done well to share with me in my present difficulty" (Phil. 4:13). This verse is often taken out of context, especially when verse 14 is ignored. The "present difficulty" Paul mentions is that he is writing this letter from prison, jailed for spreading the good news of Jesus. He understands firsthand about enduring hardship and remaining content in all circumstances through Christ's strength.

Whatever you're waiting for or enduring, I pray that your belief in Him grows stronger. May you find unexpected blessings sprinkled throughout the very act of believing. Perhaps the true miracle is the unshakable peace and contentment that sustain us during life's storms.

In the waiting, continue to focus on what you've been learning through this journey. Keep your eyes on Jesus, resisting the urge to fixate solely on the outcome you long for. Rather than measuring His love by whether or not your prayer is answered the way you hope, anchor your heart in the truth of who He is—unchanging, sovereign, and always present. A key takeaway is not just that the woman in our story reached out in faith but also Who she reached out to.

Take deliberate steps toward Jesus. Keep asking for healing, praying for the miracle, and bringing your burdens before Him (Luke 18:1). Our God is approachable, compassionate, and eager to hear from His children. He invites us to present our requests to Him, not as a formula for getting what we want but as an act of trust that deepens our relationship with Him (Phil. 4:6).

> Our God is approachable, compassionate, and eager to hear from His children.

As you wait, expand your understanding of His vast power and goodness. Search the Scriptures and reflect on the ways He has been faithful, both in the lives of others and in your own. Allow the wonder of who He is to fill you with awe, stirring a reverence so deep that it brings you to your knees before Him.

Receive your identity as His beloved daughter. Your worth is not measured by whether or not your prayer is answered in the way you expect. You are seen, known, and deeply loved, not because of your faith but because of His grace. Hold fast to this truth, letting it sustain you no matter what the future holds.

PRAYER

Dear God,

Thank You for being a God I can come to with all my questions, requests, and raw emotions. Thank You for allowing me to come to You just as I am. Lord, I look around and see so much need within my life, the lives of those I love, and the world around me. The deepest burdens on my heart right now are ________________. I ask You to move, to heal, and to bring transformation.

I stand expectantly, hoping for miracles, but I also ask that You build my faith in Your goodness, in both the waiting and independent of the outcome. Please give me contentment in the storms and Your peace that exceeds anything I can understand.

God, You spoke through Your prophet Isaiah centuries ago, reminding us that Your ways are higher than ours, Your thoughts beyond our understanding (Isa. 55:8–9). I'm grateful for the reminder of Your majesty and vast wisdom, but I also find it challenging when I can't fully comprehend Your ways. Please help me fill the gap between my understanding and Yours with unwavering belief and faith in Your perfect plan.

You know the miracle I am longing for, Lord. While I wait, please open my heart to see glimpses of You, even in the pain. Reveal Your presence to me, and use this season to shape me more into the woman You've created me to be. I trust You. I believe You. And when doubt arises, help my unbelief. You are worthy of my praise!

In Jesus's name, amen.

Reflect & Respond

How have unanswered prayers impacted your faith? Have they drawn you closer to God, created doubt, or both?

What does it mean to you that belief itself is a blessing? Can you recall a time when your faith carried you through even when circumstances didn't change? What internal blessings have you received?

Activity: Write a raw, honest letter to God about what you're still waiting for. Pour out your heart. Be specific about the miracle you long for, the feelings it stirs, and the questions you're afraid to voice. Then write a second letter from your future self who has walked through the waiting with God. What would you say about how God met you in the middle of it? Follow up with prayer, using the following prompt: *God, I release my grip on the outcome of ______________. I place it in Your hands, not because I no longer care but because I trust You more than what I think I need. Help me live surrendered, not resigned—hopeful, not hardened.*

Chapter Twelve

Her Voice

I once attended a fashion show fundraiser for a local nonprofit Christian counseling center that provides biblically based therapy for women and girls on a sliding cost scale. Their mission is to make counseling accessible to those who might otherwise be unable to afford it. The event was designed to raise funds and awareness, thereby eliminating financial barriers to receiving care.

The atmosphere was vibrant and full of energy, but what made the night unforgettable were the stories woven throughout the evening. Three videos were played at different points in the program, each featuring a woman who had once been a client. In raw, heartfelt testimonies, they shared the deep struggles that led them to seek counseling, their inability to afford it, and how therapy became a crucial part of their healing. Each video ended with a radiant smile, evidence of their growth, strength, and resilience.

But what made these stories even more powerful was the moment of revelation. These very women served as some of the models that night. As they confidently walked the runway, their courage took center stage. They weren't just survivors; they were living testimonies of hope, boldly stepping forward, figuratively and literally, as reflections of God's redemptive work.

As the crowd erupted in cheers at the end of the event, a realization settled deep within me. There was a common thread woven throughout each of their stories. Every woman shared that through healing she had found her voice.

Through healing she had found her voice.

One of the greatest gifts we receive through God's healing is the courage to use our voice.

Oh, how this truth tugged at my heart, reminding me of our redeemed woman who encountered Jesus. Think back on her story. The woman has just touched Jesus's robe, and her body has experienced miraculous healing. Then Jesus stopped. He didn't have to. Jairus was desperate for Jesus to reach his dying daughter in time. I can only imagine the tension and anxiety in Jairus's heart and the pressing need to keep moving. And yet Jesus paused to ask what must have seemed like a ridiculous question: "Who touched Me?"

If all He wanted was to acknowledge the woman, He could have done that with a glance, a knowing smile, or a subtle nod and continued on His way. But He didn't.

I often find the deepest meaning in Jesus's actions when

considering what else He could have done yet chose not to. So why did He stop? What purpose did it serve?

Jesus wanted her voice to be heard.

Jesus wanted her voice to be heard.

This beautiful woman had been silenced too long. The years of pain, isolation, and shame had robbed her voice and pushed her into the shadows of society. Jesus didn't stop at her physical healing, and He didn't stop after calling her out of hiding. He was calling her out to share her story.

We can't miss this. Cultural norms dictated that women remain quiet in public, unseen and unheard. Yet again we see Jesus breaking societal expectations, prioritizing love over the Law. Not only is this woman drawn out of darkness, but she is in the spotlight. And what is she speaking about? She is revealing the very condition that had been the root of her suffering. This is not a woman speaking from humiliation but from elation. Hear her voice. It doesn't quake with shame or hesitate with insecurity. She is bold. Unencumbered. Free.

Your voice matters too. I don't know the life circumstances that made you hide or the source of your belief that your voice isn't valuable or needed in this world. But your story is beautiful and deserves to be shared. Don't wait until your story feels complete; it's always unfolding. Don't silence your story out of fear that it's less powerful than the story of the woman next to you. When we encounter the goodness of God and realize we can no longer stay hidden, our natural response is to share our story.

Jesus is calling you to share your voice. It's time to break your silence. This isn't about drawing attention to yourself; it's about shining a spotlight on the evidence of God's grace, power, and love.

If sharing your story feels intimidating, perhaps fear has kept you silent for too long. Maybe doubts are already creeping in. "I don't know what to say. I am not eloquent with my words." But of course you are limited. You're human. Could it be that God wants to use your voice for that very reason, so *He* is the one glorified and renowned? Maybe He chose your voice because it's imperfect so His power, not yours, is revealed.

You're not alone in feeling unsure. Even the prophet Moses, one of the greatest leaders in history, wrestled with the same doubts. Consider this conversation God had with him after He instructed him to speak to Pharoah, the unyielding king of Egypt who had enslaved the Israelites.

> *But Moses pleaded with the Lord, "O Lord, I'm not very good with words. I never have been, and I'm not now, even though you have spoken to me. I get tongue-tied, and my words get tangled."*
>
> *Then the Lord asked Moses, "Who makes a person's mouth? Who decides whether people speak or do not speak, hear or do not hear, see or do not see? Is it not I, the Lord? Now go! I will be with you as you speak, and I will instruct you in what to say."*
>
> —Exod. 4:10–12

Moses hesitated to use his voice and even attempted to explain to God why His plan was flawed. But notice God didn't entertain his excuses. Instead, he offered a powerful, three-part promise that is true for you today.

"Now go!" No more excuses, no more hesitation. Stop overthinking it and act.

"I will be with you as you speak." You are never alone when you speak the truth God has written on your life.

"I will instruct you in what to say." He will equip you. You don't have to have the perfect words, just a willing heart.

This is a promise we can stand on. Sharing your story doesn't have to happen on a stage with a microphone. Most often, it happens in everyday moments around a table, in a prayer group, or across a coffee shop booth. The power isn't in the platform; it's in the willingness. Be ready. Keep your heart open. When the time comes, God will prompt your heart and open your mouth.

> *I will tell everyone about your righteousness. All day long I will proclaim your saving power, though I am not skilled with words. I will praise your mighty deeds, O Sovereign Lord. I will tell everyone that you alone are just.*
>
> —Ps. 71:15–16)

So imagine her, this once-isolated woman who shared her story that day—not hidden, not hushed, not ashamed.

Her head high, her voice echoed in the ears of those who once overlooked her. She was heard. She was seen. And in sharing her truth, she became a vessel of God's glory.

That is the invitation extended to you. You, too, are meant to rise, speak, and reflect the redemptive love of the One who called you out. Don't wait for perfection. Your voice is powerful because of the grace that fills your imperfections. Like the woman in our story, you have a voice that needs to be heard, created to share a story worth living.

PRAYER

Dear God,

I have been quiet, and You already know the reasons why. But I hear you calling me out of my silence. Because of Your goodness, I am no longer hidden. I recognize that sharing my story is part of my healing. Guide me as I reflect on this chapter and consider my testimony and the ways You are wanting to use my voice. Open my eyes to Your hand in my life and guide my words as I shape my story. Show me how I've silenced myself, and give me the courage to break free.

You've created me to be free and bold with my voice. It's not about me; I will bring You glory and bring the works You've done in my life into the light. I hear You and ask You to give me the same promise You once gave

Moses. Be with me; give me the words to say. I surrender as Your vessel. Speak through me.

In Jesus's name, amen.

Reflect & Respond

You've already been crafting your story as you follow Jesus through this journey and record your thoughts in your journal. And there is so much more to come. I'm so excited for you. I know God has even more to reveal to you. Pause and reflect on the following prompts.

How would you describe your life before encountering God?

What circumstances were you facing, and what emotions did this stir?

How has God's goodness impacted your life? If you're unsure, flip back to your previous journal entries as you've been journeying through this book. Do you see a common thread emerging?

What has been holding you back and keeping you silent? Have there been circumstances where you've avoided speaking up? What thoughts, circumstances, or objections silenced you?

Who is a safe person God is calling you to speak with? Before the conversation, imagine Jesus telling you, "'Now go! I will be with you as you speak, and I will instruct you in what to say'" (Exod. 4:12).

Note:

Working through these prompts is a powerful first step in putting words around your Story Worth Living. As you continue reading, you'll keep uncovering pieces of your story, voice, and purpose. Then, toward the end of the book, you'll find a Story Map in the Appendix—a space designed to help you gather what you've discovered and begin shaping your story in a meaningful, intentional way.

Part Four

Take Another Seat

In the previous chapter, we explored how Jesus called the healed woman to share her story, and how He calls us to do the same. But the beauty of speaking out isn't just in what it does for us. When we share our stories, we also serve others in ways we may never fully see. You never know who might be listening or how your voice might stir a heart, shift a mindset, or spark healing in someone else.

Now let's revisit this Bible story through different eyes. Step into the sandals of a bystander, someone watching from the edges. I wrote the following narrative from the perspective of a fictitious woman from the village who may have been there in the crowd that day and saw it all unfold. Her heart was moved. And her response reminds us that miracles don't just happen to one person; they often awaken something in us all.

Chapter Thirteen

A New Perspective

Begin in prayer.

Dear God,

You've already revealed so much to me just based on these few verses from Your Word. I thank You for the way You've already challenged, guided, and healed me. Now please open my mind and heart from this bystander's perspective. Make me sensitive to how I see myself in her, even if it's difficult. I am in this process of transformation and realize it's not always easy. But I trust You to guide me through it, shaping me more into the image of Jesus along the way.

In Jesus's name, amen.

A Bystander's Narrative

I wave goodbye to my friends as I step back into my home. The morning walk to the well took longer than usual today as my friends and I caught up on the town gossip. Still, these early walks are my favorite part of the day. Falling into familiar stride with my three friends, water jars swing at our sides as the quiet morning comes alive with our chatter.

During these walks, I often fall silent, letting the rhythm of our steps settle my mind. The simple connection I have with these women, forged over a lifetime, helps me shake off the stress of my marriage, my five children, and the endless household chores. These daily walks have become a lifeline for me. Sometimes we share our frustrations and disappointments. Other times we laugh and giggle until my sides hurt. Either way, I reenter my home, aching from the weight of the full jar yet feeling lighter and ready to face my day.

Today, as I call my son over to help me lift the filled water jug to pour into our wash basin, I sigh as I begin to tackle the tasks before me. My thoughts soon drift back to the conversation I had with my friends this morning.

Once again, we spoke of rumors regarding a man, Jesus of Nazareth. I must admit I am so curious about him. He has certainly been the hot topic around my village. Everyone has been sharing news of him and the wonders he performs. My mind swirls with visions of this man who has healed lepers and eaten with sinners. He is certainly causing quite a stir.

The leaders in the temple have given warnings about him, proclaiming him to be a blasphemer. Is he the man they say he is, one who disrespects our God by claiming the authority of God? But what about the miracles he performs? Some are whispering that he is the Messiah. My thoughts seem to match the pendulum motion of my broom as I sweep the floor.

I'm awakened from my reverie by a growing commotion outside. I lean my broom against the mud wall and allow my curiosity to lead me outside.

My neighbors are talking, and many are walking toward the Sea of Galilee. My dear friend's voice rises above the crowd, calling to me. "Have you heard? The man we were just speaking of this morning, Jesus of Nazareth, is on his way here, to our village. Come! Let's go see him."

Hastily tucking my hair inside my mantle and securing my baby in her sling around my neck, I allow my friend to grab my wrist and pull me into the flow of the growing crowd. The air crackles with excitement. Faces light with anticipation, and murmurs of speculation fill the air. Why is he here? What will he do? What will we see?

The baby muffles her whimpers into my chest as we tread along. I wave the stirred dust from my face. Soon, I am close to the lakeside and realize I've already missed the arrival of the boats. Fishermen and other ordinary-looking men are disembarking the boats, and I strain behind the back of a tall man in the hopes of gaining a better view of the scene. I spot Jesus not by his appearance, since he looks like any other man, but by the way his companions defer to him. His presence commands a quiet reverence. Several villagers gather around him, and I watch him patiently interact with them.

A hushed wave suddenly passes through the crowd, and I stand on tiptoes, trying to see what is happening. A man is on his knees in front of Jesus. Tears are streaming down the man's face as he pleads. "Who is that? What is he saying?" I whisper, tugging on the sleeve of a man beside me. He leans down and explains gruffly, "You know, that's Jairus, the leader in our temple. He's begging Jesus to come to his house. His daughter is near death."

A chill runs through me as I absorb the weight of the moment. This explains the desperation in the man's voice. I instinctively wrap my arm protectively around my baby girl. If she were dying, there is nothing I wouldn't do for her either.

Mesmerized, I watch as Jesus stoops low and is face to face with Jairus. There is immense compassion in his eyes as he carefully helps the man to his feet. His strong arm loops around Jairus's back, and they begin walking. I reach and grab my friend's hand as we are jostled along with the crowd and follow the two men as they exchange hushed whispers.

The crowd has thickened in a matter of minutes, and it appears our entire village has abandoned daily tasks in hopes of meeting this man or perhaps witnessing a miracle, a river of people drawn by the current of hope and wonder. My heart pounds with anticipation, my feet following, guided by the intense energy of the crowd. I'm aware of my baby, of the risk of being jostled, but I stay close to my friend, exchanging glances filled with unspoken excitement.

Suddenly, it feels like I've walked right into a wall, and I realize the man in front of me has stopped in his tracks. Jesus has stopped walking and has turned to face the crowd. "Who touched me?" he calls out. People step back, giving him space, and many look around and shake their heads in confusion. There is growing concern in Jairus's expression, and one of the men who arrived with Jesus explains that many have been touching him because so many people are following him. I assumed he'd continue the journey, but he surveyed the faces around him as an awkward silence fell.

Jesus's voice rises as he proclaims, "Someone deliberately touched me; I felt healing power go out from me."

Healing power? My heart skips a beat. What could this mean?

My friend tugs me along, and we quietly push our way through the front line of the crowd for a better view. I am about 10 feet from Jesus, so I take a moment to study him. Even though his voice is firm, I do not detect any impatience or frustration. It's as if he has all the time in the world and is determined to receive an answer to his inquiry.

His kind eyes draw me in as he pauses briefly on my face. I'm unsure how to explain it, but his face seems to display a warmth that is otherworldly. His expression is without agenda and full of unconditional love. There is no time to process the emotions sparked in me, for I realize that his attention has become focused on one face.

Following his gaze, an involuntary huff escapes my lips as I see her. My friend elbows my side as she has seen her, too, and we share an eye roll of annoyance. I know her; we were friends as children. Growing up in the same community, I remember our mothers used to walk to the well together each morning. Sometimes they'd let us tag along. I remember laughing with her as we danced, chased cats, or picked flowers. Things between us changed, however, when we became women. I was quickly married and have been blessed by God with five healthy children. The birth of my first child almost killed me, but I clearly have gained the favor of God as He spared my life and continued to fill my womb.

She, on the other hand, has been cast out by God. I don't know what she did to deserve it, but it must've been an abominable sin. Once she became a woman, she started bleeding and never stopped. She is wretched and unclean. My friends and I make it clear that she needs to stay away from us. I can't allow her to contaminate me with her vile filth. In my morning prayers, I thank God that I am not like her.

And now look what she's done. She has dared to touch this man Jesus. Oh, this awful dog! I should step in and tell Jesus who and what she is because now that she has touched him, he must go into a cleansing ceremony since she made him unclean. How dare she! Who does she think she is? She should've stayed back, away from the crowd where she belongs. Wait until I tell all my friends about this. All these thoughts bounce in my mind as I wait to see how Jesus handles this disgraceful person.

I wait for his face to adjust to the realization. I wait for a look of disgust and anger, my head on a swivel as my focus bounces between the two people in front of me. My chin lifts in indignation, ready to see her get what's coming to her.

And then I witness something I can't comprehend. The fear on her face gives way to something else, something like hope, like courage. She takes a step forward on shaking legs until she falls to her knees in front of Jesus, assuming the position held by Jairus just moments prior. In a voice that strengthens with each word, she openly tells of her years of suffering. I honestly can't believe what I'm seeing. My chest heaves as I hear her explain with great anguish the pain she endured from doctors and priests who let her down. My heart pounds in my head as she speaks of the crushing weight of isolation, the wounds inflicted not just by her body but by the scorn of people like me.

I feel acid rise in my throat as I am faced with her agony on full display, a despair I have refused to see for 12 years, agony I contributed to. Her vulnerability cracks my heart open.

There, on her knees, gazing at Jesus's face, she smiles through her sobs. Speaking louder now, determined for all to hear, she proclaims, "I am healed! My bleeding has stopped!"

How can this be? Could it be true? I know if I wasn't witnessing this myself, I don't think I would believe it. This ordinary-looking man has the power to heal with a simple touch! Who is this?! Yes, he appears ordinary, but he is clearly anything but. There is something extraordinary about him that cannot be denied or defined. Could the rumors be true? Is this man the Messiah that my ancestors and I have been anticipating for hundreds of years?

I look at Jesus, searching for some sign of judgment, but there is none. Instead, He smiles gently and says, "Daughter, your faith has made you well. Go in peace."

I gasp. Daughter! He called her daughter.

A sob escapes my lips, and the tears I'd been holding back cascade down my cheeks. My ears do not deceive me. My mouth hangs open as I can't seem to get enough oxygen. Daughter! This holy man who has the power to heal just called this woman daughter. The ground suddenly feels less solid beneath my feet as memories flood my heart, and I'm overwhelmed by the contrast with how I have treated her.

Over the years, I have called her a dog, unclean, and evil. I compared her to tax collectors and Samaritans. To her face and behind her back, I've belittled and judged her. I was convinced she was outside of God's will and grace. I accepted the guidance of religious leaders who warned of contamination. They said it was her sin that caused such a physical condition, and it was wrong to associate with her. I was convinced I was better, more righteous. I was convinced I was protecting myself and my home.

I feel like I'm outside myself, flooded with this new truth. How could I have been so wrong for so long?

I'm unaware that the crowd has started to shift and follow Jesus and Jairus once more until my friend tugs at my sleeve. She glances at the woman, shrugs, and tells me to hurry so we can follow and see what happens next. How does she seem so unfazed? My feet remain rooted as I watch her turn and continue with the crowd.

It feels like I'm under water, and I barely register the voices of the crowd as they jostle around me. My baby stirs in her sling, shifting for comfort, and I look at her as fresh tears fall from my face. I glance back and forth between my baby and this woman, and I'm flooded with both shame and gratitude. Just this morning, I was complaining about my family, complaining that I have five children and a devoted husband I have been taking for granted. I've had the nerve to grumble and rant over the most trivial of things. Overwhelmed with conviction, I am faced with the contrast of my life with this woman who has been denied the blessings of marriage, motherhood, and friendship.

Finally, the crowd moves along, and only two of us—the woman and I—remain. Now I am the one who trembles as she senses my presence and looks over her shoulder at me. Our eyes connect for the first time in years, and I can't find the words. How do I begin to express my exposed shame? Do adequate words even exist to build a large enough bridge over the chasm that my pride has created? I know I do not deserve her forgiveness. I have no right to even ask for it. My remorse eats at my stomach as I force myself to maintain eye contact.

I expect to see anger. I steel myself for harsh words or a cold shoulder. I know that is what I deserve. But I'm shocked at what I see. There is a tender, small smile on her face. I see unconditional love. How could this be? That is when I realize her face mirrors the expressions I just witnessed on the face of Jesus. How stunning! How absolutely powerful and beautiful! It's as if she is now able to share the same love that she just received from Jesus. Is that even possible? Yes! It's her transformation on full display. She absorbed so much love from Him that it is now flowing from her, and I am humbled to be on the receiving end.

She absorbed so much love from Him that it is now flowing from her.

Now I can no longer stand, and I allow the fear and apprehension to slide away as I crumble to my knees in front of her and we fall into each other's arms. I wordlessly express regret and remorse as I hug my old friend. She grips me as we smile, sob, and laugh in amazement. In the same way she recognized her immediate healing, I trust that my forgiveness is just as immediate, even for the pain I helped cause. Eventually, we help each other up as gleeful laughter continues, and we turn arm in arm to walk back into town, knowing we will never be the same.

Reflect & Respond

In the pages that follow, we will pull a few of the major themes that have been revealed by walking in the shoes of this bystander. But for now, take some time to explore your initial reaction.

What emotions does this narrative stir in you?

In what ways do you personally identify with the bystander? How do you see yourself in her?

Think of a time you witnessed the work of Jesus in another person's life. How did that experience impact you?

Chapter Fourteen

Conviction Calls

There were countless people fortunate enough to witness the teachings and miracles of Jesus. And just like the bleeding woman, each had their struggles, responsibilities, worldviews, and personalities. Journeying through this scene with our fictitious bystander allows us to recognize Jesus's profound impact on those who had a front-row seat to His power. Yet just as some in the crowd touched Him and remained unchanged, we can assume some carried on with the processional, unmoved by the woman weeping on her knees as she proclaimed her transformation.

I see myself in this bystander. Perhaps you do too. Her experience exposes uncomfortable tendencies that are difficult to admit. I can identify with her apathy, judgment, and pride. I, too, have been so consumed by the everyday responsibilities of my life that I fail to notice the pain of others around me. I've taken one fragment of someone's story and stretched it into an assumption, boxing her in so I could set her aside and move on.

But the grace of Jesus reaches me here too. Even in my blindness, He sees me. Even in my hardness, He softens me. He uses these moments to open my eyes and tenderize my heart, expanding my understanding of His boundless goodness and grace.

Even in my blindness, He sees me. Even in my hardness, He softens me.

I have a vivid memory from when I was around 10 years old. It was a beautiful day, and I was playing in my front yard with my friend Jennifer. My childhood home sat on a curve at the bottom of a hill. As we played, I noticed a woman on a walk coming down the street toward us.

This was the 1980s, the era of Richard Simmons' *Sweatin' to the Oldies*, and she looked the part. Dressed in neon colors with matching sweatbands, she was fully committed to her workout. Her hips swung with each step, and her arms pumped with exaggerated enthusiasm as she power-walked her heart out.

When I spotted her, I thought she was hilarious. In my immature attempt to get a laugh out of my friend Jennifer, I began to mock her. I mimicked her movements, prancing around the yard in an over-the-top imitation. As she came closer, I noticed her name printed boldly across the front of her shirt in all caps varsity font: PAULA. That was all the encouragement I needed. With a sing-songy, obnoxious voice, I called out, "Paaauuulllaa! Paaaauuullaa!" over and over, delighting in Jennifer's laughter.

Paula walked right past us, her head held high, never

acknowledging my taunts. As she walked out of sight, Jennifer and I moved on to our next game without giving her another thought.

Later that afternoon, after Jennifer had gone home, my doorbell rang. To my delight, it was Kimberly, a girl who had recently moved to our street. I'd played with her a few times and was thrilled to see she'd come over. But my excitement faded the moment I saw the look on her face.

With her hands on her hips and eyes blazing, she glared at me. "How dare you. That was my mom you were making fun of. I never want to see you again."

Her words hit me like a punch to the gut. My mouth fell open as realization crashed over me, forcing me to see my actions for what they were—thoughtless, unkind, and cruel.

I stammered an apology, but she had already turned away. "I didn't know she was your mom!" I called after her, desperate to make it right. But even as the words left my mouth, I heard how hollow they sounded. Did it matter that I didn't know? Would it have made my actions less cruel?

Even as an immature 10-year-old, I understood the painful truth. It shouldn't have mattered whether Paula was Kimberly's mom. She was someone's mom. More importantly, she was someone, a person who didn't deserve to be mocked and ridiculed.

Years later, the shame still stings when I remember that moment. But it also taught me a powerful lesson. Sometimes we don't care how we treat someone until we know who they belong to. You see, I didn't care that I had mistreated Paula, but I was heartbroken to learn I had mistreated Kimberly's mom.

> Sometimes we don't care how we treat someone until we know who they belong to.

That day I learned a hard truth about how easy it is to dehumanize someone until we're forced to see them through a different lens. And perhaps that's what happened to the bystander that day with Jesus. For years, she went along with the rest of society, treating the bleeding woman like an outcast, justifying her cruelty as self-preservation. She was firm in her belief that she was better than. Perhaps she never gave the woman's suffering a second thought until she heard Jesus call her "daughter."

Before we rush past the bystander, let's pause. Because if we're honest, she lives in us too. We all carry pride. We all struggle with judgment. We all have a tendency to compare, elevate ourselves, and look down on others. But Jesus, in His wisdom, told a powerful parable that gets straight to the heart of this struggle.

> *Two men went to the temple to pray. One was a Pharisee, and the other was a despised tax collector. The Pharisee stood by himself and prayed this prayer: "I thank You, God, that I am not like other people—cheaters, sinners, adulterers. I'm certainly not like that tax collector! I fast twice a week, and I give You a tenth of my income."*

> *But the tax collector stood at a distance and dared not even lift his eyes to heaven as he prayed. Instead, he beat his chest in sorrow, saying, "O God, be merciful to me, for I am a sinner." I tell you, this sinner, not the Pharisee, returned home justified before God. For those who exalt themselves will be humbled, and those who humble themselves will be exalted.*
>
> —Luke 18:10–14

Jesus was an incredible storyteller and used this gift to reveal the heart of the Father as He also exposed truths about our character. This particular parable illuminates God's focus on the posture of our hearts. Compare the sightline of these two men. The Pharisee's sight is horizontal, looking at the others around him. He's consumed with comparison and exalting himself. The tax collector was focused on his shortcomings, so much so that he couldn't lift his eyes toward heaven. Our God longs for humility, genuine repentance, and a heart that cries out, "God, be merciful to me." Like me that day in the yard and like the bystander watching Jesus, the Pharisee didn't see his own pride. He measured his worth by looking down on others. But the tax collector? He knew his need for mercy.

God's conviction isn't condemnation; it's an invitation to transformation. When He reveals the hidden corners of our hearts, we have two choices: resist and retreat or open ourselves to His refining work. Conviction can be a tough pill to swallow, but it's an immeasurable gift. When God brings these areas to light, we must silence the whispers of shame. So let's embrace His loving correction, knowing He uses it to shape us and remind us of our true identity in Christ.

> God's conviction isn't condemnation; it's an invitation to transformation.

As Hebrews 12:11 tells us, "No discipline is enjoyable while it is happening—it's painful! But afterward there will be a peaceful harvest of right living for those who are trained in this way."

The more I fall in love with Jesus, the more I welcome His conviction. Why? Because I know it's for my good. It's worth the promise of His harvest of righteousness and peace. Imagine a heart surgeon about to operate. No one wants surgery. It's painful, messy, and difficult. But when you trust the surgeon's skill and know the operation will save your life, you submit to it. In the same way, our Heavenly Father desires to shape us more into the image of Jesus. He is the ultimate heart surgeon, and when we trust Him, we willingly lay our hearts open on His table, asking Him to do His refining work in us.

PRAYER

Dear God,

Thank You for this opportunity to walk in a bystander's shoes amid Your interaction with this woman. May I not be like the other bystanders who went on their way, unchanged.

Father, I know there is self-righteousness in me. Break my heart for what breaks Yours. While the exposure will be painful, I lay my heart open to You now. Give me the courage to honestly reflect and the confidence to know You will use this time to work Your power in my heart.

In Jesus's name, amen.

Reflect & Respond

Who is your "Paula"? Who have you dismissed, judged, or ridiculed? Ask God to bring them to mind and show you the necessary next steps.

Who are "those people" to you? Is there a group you've mentally categorized, people you've dismissed, criticized, or labeled without knowing their stories? What assumptions have you made about them, and how might God be inviting you to see them differently?

How has the power of groupthink influenced your treatment of another person? For example, the bleeding woman's community mistreated her and made it easier for this bystander to justify her behavior. What would it take to break free from that mindset?

What does it look like to welcome the heart surgeon? What would you change if you knew God's conviction was a sign of His deep love for you? What areas of your life will you surrender to Him today, even if the process feels uncomfortable?

Chapter Fifteen

Connection Calls

When we allow the conviction of Christ to transform us, we'll know it. There is a marked difference, a new awakening in how we see the world and ourselves.

One evening I was out to eat with friends when a woman walked into the restaurant with a man I assumed was her husband. Her attire caught my attention. Let's just say it wasn't something I would wear. She had quite a bit of skin showing for my more conservative taste. My instinct was to lean over to my friend sitting beside me and make a snide remark about the woman's clothing. But before the words left my mouth, I paused.

Since immersing myself in the story of Jesus and the bleeding woman, I've been praying for Him to transform me from the inside out. I've asked Him to give me His eyes for the world around me, starting with my own heart. In this moment in the restaurant, the Holy Spirit wasted no time convicting me. Shifting my gaze inward, I wrestled with my thoughts: *Gee, Amy. Is that really who you want to be, someone willing to put down another woman just to get a laugh?*

I almost became the woman I've worked so hard not to be—the one who whispers insults behind cupped hands, who uses sarcasm to mask her own insecurities. But Jesus interrupted me, not with shame, but with invitation—"See her the way I do."

But Jesus interrupted me, not with shame, but with invitation—"See her the way I do."

As the conversation and bustle of dinner continued around me, I sat back, letting the weight of the realization sink in. Instead of ridiculing, I offered a silent prayer and thanked God for stopping me before my words caused harm. This situation could have had a very different outcome. Jesus wasn't just stopping me from speaking; He was teaching me something far deeper about how I see and treat others.

When I ask to see the world through the eyes of Jesus, that's what I'll receive. I believe this is one of God's favorite requests to grant. As soon as conviction struck, I suddenly saw this woman differently. I no longer saw a woman I wanted to ridicule; instead, I saw a beautiful, confident woman enjoying a meal with her husband. I saw someone who had likely taken time to pick out her outfit, apply her makeup, and prepare for a special occasion. A smile of appreciation replaced my initial criticism, and instead of tearing her down, I paused to offer a silent prayer for her and her marriage.

Jesus also shut my mouth out of love and respect for my friend. When we choose to enter into true sisterhood with another woman, a responsibility accompanies that connection. Friendship centered on Christ carries unwritten rules and boundaries to safeguard. I don't want to be a person who spreads darkness into someone else's soul. Guarding my heart also requires me to guard other hearts as well. We should commit to uplifting, not corrupting, one another.

Then Jesus gently reminded me, "Hey, that's My daughter." And I knew He meant all three of us—that woman, my friend, and me. As I looked at the woman across the restaurant, I no longer saw an outfit; I saw a soul. I saw a human being for whom Jesus went to the cross, someone lovingly knit together by the hands of our Creator. I saw His daughter whom He cherished beyond measure. Glancing over at my friend as we continued in conversation at our table, I saw a woman I admire and respect, someone I would never intentionally harm. I saw another daughter of Jesus and felt the honor of walking beside her in this life, knowing that entails my commitment to do all I can to shine His light into her heart and protect it from any negativity I might be tempted to pass along.

And then there was me. In that quiet moment, I felt Jesus's loving gaze—His proud Father moment when His daughter grasped an important life lesson. He knew I got it, and a knowing smile crossed my lips. I could imagine Him leaning over to nudge a nearby angel as He pointed at me and said: "Hey, that's My daughter." When we see the world through the eyes of Jesus, it becomes nearly impossible to be unkind.

When we see the world through the eyes of Jesus, it becomes nearly impossible to be unkind.

I thought again about the woman in Scripture and how long she had lived under the weight of judgment. I wondered how many women had glanced at her the way I initially looked at the woman across the restaurant, with quick judgment and quiet contempt. I wondered how many leaned in to whisper about her, never pausing to understand her.

But Jesus didn't look at her that way. He treated her with dignity. He saw her whole. That same Jesus meets me in my moments of judgment, not to shame me but to heal me and help me see others the way He does, with compassion and connection. In that restaurant moment, I realized I had a choice. I could be like the crowd who overlooked her pain, or I could be like Jesus—someone who chooses to see and elevate others with love.

Following Jesus and allowing Him to transform us doesn't keep us from being negative and cruel. His love doesn't settle for neutrality or passivity. It propels us forward. He elevates us by allowing His love to flow through us to the world around us.

It's clear throughout Scripture that Jesus served to elevate the value of women. Seeing how He broke through cultural norms makes me love Him all the more and makes me incredibly proud to be a woman. As His followers, we can all unite in compassionate sisterhood with the confidence that we don't have to put each other down to lift ourselves up. Jesus has already lifted us higher than we could ever lift ourselves. That gives us the freedom to build each other up, recognizing that we are stronger together.

In the Apostle Paul's letter to the early church forming in the city of Thessalonica, he shared, "So encourage each other and build each other up, just as you are already doing" (1 Thess. 5:11). I love the imagery embedded in his words "build each other up." Our words are like hammers; they have the power to tear down or build up. Think about it. When we are using a hammer for demolition purposes, we don't have to be very precise. We can sling it around, be reckless, and still get the job done. Similarly, words spoken in haste or out of insecurity can cause lasting damage.

The opposite is also true. When we use a hammer to build, we have to be careful and deliberate. Builders don't just throw materials together; they measure, place, and secure everything with care. It takes forethought and attention. Our words should do the same. When spoken with intention and love, they have the power to lift, encourage, and heal. We have the power to unite and have a significant impact on the quality of someone's life.

I've experienced this firsthand. More times than I'd like

to admit, I've spoken harshly about myself. I have criticized my appearance, my abilities, and my worth. But I have a friend who refuses to let me tear myself down. Whenever I say something negative, she looks me in the eyes and says, "Hey, don't talk about my friend that way." It always stops me in my tracks. At that moment, she's not just correcting me; she's protecting me. She's reminding me of the truth I so easily forget, that I am loved, valued, and seen by God. That's the sisterhood we are called to, one where we fight for each other not against each other.

We become radically unstoppable when we continuously choose to lift each other up rather than tear each other apart.

> We become radically unstoppable when we continuously choose to lift each other up rather than tear each other apart.

Friend, the more we fix our eyes on Jesus, the more He gifts us with a desire to support and encourage the women on our paths. Only then do we see other women as His daughters and, therefore, our sisters. We may not share the same DNA, but we share the same blood—the blood of Jesus. When we walk in step with Him, sisterhood becomes not just a connection but a revolution. It becomes a radically unstoppable force for healing, unity, and love in a world that desperately needs it.

PRAYER

Dear God,

I thank You for this experience. Thank You for the reminder that every woman I come in contact with is Your beautiful daughter. Thank You for elevating the value of women through your son, Jesus. Please guide me and use me to be a confident woman who freely and boldly shares Your love. Help me cultivate rich sisterhood and use my words and actions to build up other women. Forgive me for the moments I've let comparison, fear, or insecurity cloud my view of my sisters. Allow me to be one of Your agents of encouragement from this day forward.

In Jesus's name, amen.

Reflect & Respond

Can you recall a time when insecurity, pride, or comparison shaped your thoughts about another woman? How did it affect your actions? How can you receive God's grace and use it as motivation for change?

What steps can you take to ignite dangerously powerful sisterhood in your life?

Who in your life could use encouragement today? What is one specific way you can show her love, whether through a text, a prayer, or a conversation?

Part Five

The New

Part Five centers on Jesus's response to the woman's courage—her deliberate touch, her bold step out of hiding, and her willingness to share her story. He doesn't just acknowledge her; He honors her. With eyes full of tenderness, He speaks these words that must have washed over her like healing rain: "Daughter," he said to her, "your faith has made you well. Go in peace" (Luke 8:48).

In the chapters ahead, we'll unpack profound meanings embedded in Jesus's response. These aren't just words for the woman; they're words for us too. Within them are layers of healing, identity, belonging, and purpose. Let's lean in together and listen closely to what Jesus is still speaking over our lives today.

Chapter Sixteen

A New Identity

My dear friend Laurie grew up in a home where words were used as weapons. Her mother's voice, meant to be a source of love and affirmation, was instead a constant source of pain. Day after day, Laurie was bombarded with cruel, demeaning names—Stupid, Dumb, Dumb Kid. Words that should have been unthinkable from a mother's lips became the soundtrack of Laurie's childhood.

One day when Laurie was around 10 years old, she was outside playing with neighborhood friends. An obnoxious bully was riding his bike and decided to single her out. "Laurie Fart!" he taunted, over and over, his cruel twist on her name, Laurie Hart. His voice grated against her already fragile sense of self. At first, she ignored him. But with each repetition, her anger bubbled hotter until it finally boiled over.

The next time he sped past her, Laurie grabbed the back of his bike seat and yanked him off balance. The bully crashed to the ground, stunned. Before he could scramble back to his feet, Laurie leaned over and pointed a stern finger in his face. "Don't you ever call me that again!" Her voice was shaky but firm as her heart thundered in her chest. The boy blinked up at her, too shocked to speak as she turned on her heels and headed home.

Looking back, Laurie laughs at the story. It's a childhood tale that might seem amusing on the surface. But years later during a deep reflection, she had a profound realization. Why had the boy's words ignited such fierce anger while her mother's words never provoked the same response?

That's when it hit her. She fought against the bully because *she knew his words weren't true.* But the names her mother called her? She had absorbed them as facts. She never fought back because she came to believe she was stupid. She *believed* she was just a dumb kid.

This moment changed everything for Laurie. She began to understand the power of belief. It shapes and binds us, and creates the lens through which we see ourselves. A belief system isn't just a collection of thoughts; it's a pattern of thinking we accept as truth. And if we're not careful, we can build our entire identity on lies.

Maybe you can relate. Maybe you carry the heavy weight of a label pressed onto your chest, one you never asked for but somehow became yours to bear. Someone in your life has hurt you, diminished you, and made you feel small and unseen. Maybe they gaslighted you, betrayed you, or spoke words so cutting that they carved their way into your soul.

And now their damage lingers, whispering lies about who you are.

Or maybe the label you wear isn't from someone else. Perhaps it's one you gave yourself, a mark left behind by your own mistakes. We've all fallen short. We've all known the sting of regret. But some mistakes don't stay in the past where they belong. Instead, they haunt us in the quiet hours, replaying in our minds, taunting us with what-ifs and should-haves. We wrestle with guilt. We struggle to forgive ourselves. And somewhere along the way, we start to believe the worst about who we are.

If that's you, then you already have a glimpse into what life was like for the woman who reached out and touched the cloak of Jesus. For years she bore the weight of the labels the world had forced upon her. Unclean. Broken. Dirty. Disgusting. Unworthy. The voices of society didn't just name her; they defined her. And in time, those labels weren't just words spoken about her. They became the words she said to herself.

In previous chapters, we explored the woman's isolation, shame, and suffering. But beyond the physical pain, beyond the loneliness was something even deeper, something that shaped her identity. She didn't challenge the words spoken over her. She didn't fight back against the names she was given.

Why?

She believed them. They had settled into her heart and taken root in her soul—until one moment changed everything. She was there on the ground, pebbles boring into her knees as she concluded her public proclamation of her suffering, deliberate touch, and immediate healing. The air was thick with anticipation. The crowd held its breath, waiting to see how this man, a teacher and rumored healer would respond.

Then He spoke.

His first word was not a rebuke. It was not an accusation. It was not a demand for an explanation. It was a name.

"Daughter" (Luke 8:48).

We cannot overstate the seismic shift this must have produced in her heart. For years she had carried the weight of cruel and condemning labels. But in a single breath, Jesus stripped them away. With this one word—*daughter*—she was no longer just a woman desperate for healing. She was claimed. She was seen. She was wanted.

With this one word–*daughter*–she was no longer just a woman desperate for healing. She was claimed. She was seen. She was wanted.

And why does this word carry such power? Because it was accompanied by a miracle. Jesus's authority over her healing was undeniable, but so was His authority over her identity. The Savior of the world, the One who formed her in her mother's womb, who numbered the days of her life and knew every strand of hair on her head, He called her daughter. The Divine Creator, the One who placed each star in the sky, formed the land and sea, and set birds into flight, He called her daughter.

At that moment, His voice replaced every false name she believed. And that changed everything.

Just a few moments earlier, Jesus stopped and turned with a question, "Who touched Me?" (Luke 8:45). Peeling back a layer, there is an underlying question: "Who are you?" How we answer this question affects every aspect of our lives. How we view ourselves and our identity impacts our decisions, how we interact with others, steps we take in our careers, how we care for our bodies—*everything*.

I don't know the labels you've carried. Some have been whispered over you; others were shouted. Some were handed to you by people you trusted, while others came from your mistakes. But the hardest part? These labels have settled so deeply into your belief system that you barely recognize them as lies anymore.

But it's time—time to refuse their hold on you, time to follow Laurie-not-Fart's example and get angry. You have a purpose and an identity as a daughter of the King of kings to claim. So how long will you let these false names hold you back? What are these labels costing you?

> You have a purpose and an identity as a daughter of the King of kings to claim.

Today is the day they come off for good.

Close your eyes for a moment. Picture yourself standing before the cross. Reach out and feel the rough, splintered wood beneath your fingertips. Touch the symbol of suffering, of death. Now turn. Beside you stands Jesus. His eyes are filled with compassion, patience, and an unshakable love. He doesn't rush you. He waits.

Tear off the old labels you've carried for so long. Maybe it stings as they peel away from your heart. Maybe part of you hesitates. But then, with trembling hands, you press them to the beam of the cross.

And Jesus, He nods. Without hesitation, He gives His life to forever remove your stains and wash you white as snow by claiming you as His own.

So the next time you feel haunted by the labels of your past, picture them hanging there, nailed to the cross behind Jesus. If you ever want them back, you'll have to ask Him for them.

I can promise you Jesus would rather die than give them back to you.

Because that's exactly what He did.

PRAYER

Dear God,

Calling You Father now carries a deeper, more profound meaning. Not only are You my Creator, but I am Your daughter—redeemed, held, and claimed. I am Yours.

You know how hard it is for me to fully accept this truth. The false labels I've carried for so long have shaped my identity. But today, I see them as the lies they've always been. The image of them adhered to the cross resonates deeply within me. And yet I know the whispers will come again. The enemy will tempt me to doubt, just as he did with Eve, saying, "Did God really say?" (Gen. 3:1).

So, Father, when the lies return, strengthen me to stand on Your truth.

"For you are all children of God through faith in Christ Jesus" (Gal. 3:26).

"See how very much our Father loves us, for he calls us his children, and that is what we are!" (1 John 3:1).

"You received God's Spirit when he adopted you as his own children. Now we call him, 'Abba, Father.' For his Spirit joins with our spirit to affirm that we are God's children. And since we are his children, we are his heirs. In fact, together with Christ we are heirs of God's glory" (Rom. 8:15–17).

"I have called you by name; you are mine" (Isa. 43:1).

"You are a chosen people. You are royal priests, a holy nation, God's very own possession" (1 Pet. 2:9).

Thank You for arming me with these truths. What an honor to be Your daughter. You alone have the authority to name me. You alone define who I am.

God, walk with me as I step into this time of reflection. Reveal the places I have believed lies, and replace them with Your unshakable truth. Let this be a moment of transformation.

I love You.

In Jesus's name, amen.

Reflect & Respond

On a fresh page in your journal, write the title "False Labels" across the top. Then examine and record all the lies you've believed about yourself. Be honest. This may feel difficult and raw, but it's a necessary step toward healing and growth.

Next, take a bold marker and write "Daughter" across your list in large, clear, undeniable print. Pause and look at it. What emotions rise within you?

Sit with this truth for a moment. You are not defined by lies. You are defined by the One who calls you His.

Now consider this: What fears or doubts hold you back from believing it?

What would it look like to walk in the confidence of being God's daughter every single day?

Let this be a turning point. The old labels no longer define you. Your identity is secure in Him.

Chapter Seventeen

Mistaken Identity

My grandfather (Pawpaw) was quite a character—stern and formidable with a presence that commanded attention. As a little girl, I felt a healthy fear and a deep sense of safety in his home. His signature line, delivered with a dramatic fist shake, was, "I run this house with an iron hand!" And he did. But behind the bluster were moments of quiet tenderness. Sitting under the big oak tree in his backyard, we shelled butter beans in companionable silence. It was in those moments I felt both small and deeply seen.

Pawpaw also had a playful streak. He loved giving people nicknames and proudly bore one of his own—Captain Midnight. It was even stamped on his personalized license plate. At his funeral when I was in high school, someone asked me how he got the nickname. I shared what I'd always believed to be true, that he earned it during his service in World War

II. He told me his fellow soldiers gave it to him during their time in the Army, and I had carried that version of the story ever since.

As I finished relaying the tale, my aunt who was standing nearby burst into laughter and quickly corrected me. "That's not where his nickname came from." According to her, Captain Midnight had nothing to do with his military service and everything to do with the late-night poker games he played with friends at the local Elks Lodge. My grandmother would let Pawpaw have it if he wasn't home by midnight. His buddies thought it was hilarious and thus gave him the nickname that stayed with him the remainder of his life. I suppose the version he told me was a little more heroic and curated for his granddaughter's sake.

That moment at the funeral stayed with me, not because I felt deceived but because it reminded me how easily our understanding of someone can be shaped by the narrative we're given or the one they want us to believe. For all those years, I carried a false version of the story that felt true to me.

This is also the case with how many of us view God. We carry assumptions or incomplete stories about who God is, stories shaped by what we were told, how we were raised, or our experiences with earthly fathers or authority figures. Sometimes the image we carry is accurate. Other times, it's incomplete at best and misleading at worst.

For some of us, calling God "Father" is complicated. If our earthly fathers were absent, easily angered, inconsistent, untrustworthy, or even abusive, imagining God as anything different can be challenging. It might feel easier to relate to Him as Judge or Creator, as One who is distant, powerful, and in control, but not as a loving, present Dad.

Many of us carry silent wounds from men who were supposed to protect and guide us. Maybe your father was physically or emotionally absent. Maybe he was harsh, critical, or quick to anger. Perhaps love felt conditional, something you had to earn by performing well or staying out of trouble. Maybe he was silent when you desperately needed guidance, or his approval always felt out of reach.

When your earliest picture of "father" is tied to pain, it distorts how you imagine your Heavenly Father. We project those disappointments onto God, assuming He must also be distant, demanding, or uninterested in our hearts. And over time, our view of Him becomes shaped more by what we lack than by who He truly is.

> God is not a projection of your earthly father. He is the perfection of fatherhood.

But God is not a projection of your earthly father. He is the perfection of fatherhood. A good father is more than just an authority figure. He is present, offering protection and providing steady, unconditional love. While he does discipline, it is never to harm. His corrections come from a place of love and a desire for what is best for his child. He is approachable yet deeply respected, creating an environment where his children feel safe and seen.

A good father delights in his children, inviting them into

his presence rather than intimidating them. He speaks the truth without shaming, offering both strength and softness. He makes room for failures without withholding love, building a foundation of security where his children can grow and flourish.

God is that kind of Father. He is not threatened by your doubts, your wounds, or your wandering heart. His arms offer correction and comfort, and His presence longs to fill you with a sense of security, to make you feel wanted and known.

Return to a pivotal moment in the encounter the healed woman had with Jesus. We've explored the significance of her restored identity. But there's something deeper tucked inside Jesus's words.

When Jesus called her daughter, He wasn't just declaring a new identity for her. He was declaring a new *relationship*. Consider how strange this might have seemed to onlookers. Jesus was likely around 30 to 33 years old during His ministry. Depending on the age when her condition began, this woman may have been in her late 20s or even older. So why would a man only a few years her senior refer to her as daughter?

He was speaking on behalf of Someone else. In that moment, Jesus wasn't just performing a miracle. He was revealing the heart of the Father. He was saying, "You are not just healed. You are Mine. You are welcomed, chosen, and named. You have a Father."

I don't know the cases of mistaken identity you've carried about yourself or God, but it's time to allow Him to chip away at that confusion. Just as you've removed the false labels you've worn, it's time to remove those you've placed on God. Let Him give you eyes to recognize Him as your good Father. I am deeply sorry if you carry wounds from an earthly father figure, but don't let his shortcomings define how you see your perfect Heavenly Father any longer.

Approach your time in reflection with an open, curious heart.

PRAYER

Dear God,

Thank You for Your goodness, sovereignty, and steadfastness. You know all the ways I've misunderstood Your role as my Father, and You already know the root of my confusion. Thank You for raising my awareness. Help me to continue to see You as the Father You truly are. Guide me as I explore the following questions with You in my journaling and reflection. I see this as a pivotal opportunity to deepen my connection with You. Open my eyes to Your truth. I trust You.

In Jesus's name, amen.

Reflect & Respond

Reflect on the relationships with father figures in your life—your biological father, stepfather, grandfather, father-in-law, older brother, coach, teacher, or anyone else who played that role. How did these relationships shape or confuse your view of God as Father? Consider moments where you might have experienced pain or disappointment. Is there any unresolved hurt that needs forgiveness or perhaps an assumption you've carried about God because of these experiences?

If the word *Father* feels heavy or distant, especially as you navigate healing from past pain, know this: God is not offended by your hesitation. He meets you right where you are. Sometimes it can be deeply healing to explore different names for God, ones that feel safe, personal, and rooted in love.

Give yourself permission to call Him what draws you closer. Maybe you connect more with Papa, Dad, Daddy, or Abba. Perhaps Shepherd, Creator, Protector, or simply God feels like a more honest starting point right now.

Take a moment to sit quietly and consider this: What name for God feels like a warm invitation? Trust that God is fine with whatever title you choose because He cares more about your authentic attention than formal language.

Next, list qualities you would attribute to an ideal father. Consider what traits you admire in father figures or longed for in your relationship with them. Then take a moment to review your list. Can you see God in each of these qualities? Are there aspects of His character that resonate with you, or are there areas where you feel resistant to seeing Him this way? If something feels hard to accept, take note of it and invite God to reveal Himself in that area as you continue to grow in your relationship with Him.

How would your time with God change if you could fully view Him as the perfect Father? Imagine what it would be like to see Him as someone who is always present, gentle, guiding, and unwavering in His love for you. How might that change the way you prioritize your time with Him? Would it make your time with Him feel more like a safe refuge or inspire more confidence and trust in your prayers and conversations with Him?

Chapter Eighteen

Faith

When I was younger, I enjoyed playing tennis. My family had a membership at a local pool and tennis club, and I would ride my bike to the club to meet friends or hit drills on the brick wall. Both of my parents played, and I fell in love with the game too. I was part of the women's tennis team all four years in high school.

I recall a day working with my high school coach when he pointed out something I never knew. He told me I wasn't properly gripping my racket and showed me how to line up an edge of the grip within the crease of my thumb. That rotated the racket about half an inch in my hand. I stepped over to the other side of the court, adjusting my racket as he had instructed. My coach hit a few balls my way, and I immediately felt awkward and clumsy. Just prior to that, I was consistent and confident. Now my efficiency was destroyed. I felt like a baby giraffe on new legs, dismayed as every ball I hit sailed out of bounds. I looked like it was the first time I'd ever picked up a racket.

My instinct was to switch my grip back to where I was comfortable. I'd been playing tennis for years just fine with my former grip, and I began to question my coach's advice. Surely, he could see this wasn't working.

After several failed shots, my coach could see my frustration and called me to the net for a chat. "You're having to unlearn a bad habit that served you well for a while but has now become a lid to your capability. I know this new grip feels awkward, but give it time. Trust me. It'll pay off."

We separated, and he drilled me dozens more balls. By the end of our practice session, his words were already proving true. The rest of my body's mechanics began to adjust around the proper grip, and over time my shots became more powerful and efficient than they'd ever been in my life.

In a way, the bleeding woman's encounter with Jesus was like that. She had been holding on to her own way of finding healing for so long, putting her faith in doctors and treatments that left her depleted and still unwell. Her old way of thinking—that if she just found the right doctor, she'd be okay—had become familiar and comfortable, despite the ongoing pain (Mark 5:26).

But then came a moment of desperation and determination. She took a risk and shifted her grip on what she believed would heal her. Instead of clinging to what had always been her strategy, she took a step of faith toward Jesus.

When Jesus said, "Your faith has made you well" (Luke 8:48), He wasn't saying that she healed herself. Rather, it was her willingness to change her grip on what she thought was true and reach for Him that made the difference. She let go of the old patterns and stretched toward something unfamiliar, something that seemed audacious and even awkward.

it was her willingness to change her grip on what she thought was true and reach for Him that made the difference.

The implications of this are truly limitless. Is there is a belief or habit you've been holding onto that has now become the lid to your growth? Perhaps that is exactly what God has been revealing to you as you've journeyed with Him through this experience. Breakthroughs are often just on the other side of small but powerful shifts in our thinking and behaviors.

This isn't easy. Just like my incorrect tennis racket grip, we often don't realize we are holding onto something that is hindering us. It requires faith, an open mind, and a willingness to consider the wisdom of someone who wants to help us. Jesus is that Someone. He sees our blindspots. He knows the subtle shifts that can have a profound impact.

Read through the following examples of possible thoughts that no longer serve you.

You've always believed that God loves you more when you're doing all the right things. But maybe He's inviting you to rest in His grace rather than strive to earn His favor.

You've believed that you need a clear, unmistakable sign to move forward, but perhaps God is inviting you to take small, faithful steps without seeing the whole picture. It's time to move from paralysis to trust.

You've been making decisions based on what will make others happy or comfortable. What if God is inviting you to make choices based on obedience to Him, even if it disappoints some people?

You've held onto a grudge because it feels like protection. But God might be inviting you to forgive, not because it was okay but because your heart needs to be free.

You've always thought that loving someone meant saying yes to everything. Maybe God is calling you to love them well by also protecting your own well-being.

You've been gripping certainty, firm in your opinion about that person or those people. Perhaps God is inviting you to release your long-held opinions and look at His children in a new light.

You've held tightly to beliefs about God and religious doctrine that have put limits on His power and love. He's calling you to question your grip and reconsider what is no longer serving you as His follower.

The bleeding woman didn't heal herself. She simply let go of her hope that was previously focused on the wrong source. She shifted her grip from relying on doctors to trusting in the One who could truly make her whole.

Think of it like climbing a rope. You can only go higher when you're willing to let go and reach up. Once I grew accustomed to the proper grip on my tennis racket and enjoyed the positive effects, I was never going back. The temporary discomfort and temptation to revert faded away. It would have been foolish to even consider returning to my former grip.

Think of it like climbing a rope. You can only go higher when you're willing to let go and reach up.

The same is true when we decide to release our grip on an old way of thinking or behaving and choose to reach out in faith and embrace something new. It may feel awkward at first, but when you start seeing the transformation, you will realize just how powerful that small shift can be.

A few years ago, I went through what I can only describe as a faith crisis. I was restless and wrestling, caught in a season of tension that I couldn't seem to shake. There was a stirring in my heart that lasted for months, an undeniable pull to reexamine thoughts and beliefs I once held so firmly. I finally reached a point where I knew I couldn't ignore it any longer. I had to lean in.

The word *deconstruction* gets thrown around a lot these days, but I'm not sure it fully captures my experience. Instead, it felt more like laying everything out on the table. One night, I looked toward God and pleaded, "Okay. I'm setting everything before You—my beliefs, opinions, and thoughts. Help me discern what needs to stay and what needs to go."

This was a destabilizing time in my life, and I'd be lying

if I said I wasn't scared. There was a small but nagging fear that if I put it all out there, if I truly examined everything, nothing would be left. What if I lost my faith all together in the process?

Thankfully, that wasn't the case. But in those early days, I couldn't see that clearly. I carefully, almost painstakingly, picked up each belief, held it in my hands, and lifted it to God. Is this true? Does it align with what I know about a good and loving God? Can I hold this belief and Jesus in the same grip?

As I walked through that process, something beautiful began to happen. My belief system became decluttered. Some of the old ideas I had gripped so tightly fell away, no longer compatible with the deeper understanding I was gaining. New truths became my new, proper grip, and some beliefs landed in the category of "I'm still unsure, and I'm at peace with that."

Looking back now, I see how that season reminds me of Psalm 23. God truly shepherded me through a dark valley. It was difficult yet tender, an unexpectedly intimate time with Jesus. It was as if He lovingly called me to the net, pointed out that my grip was off, and gently said, "This served you for a time, but it's become a lid to your growth."

Relearning that proper grip wasn't easy. It felt awkward, clumsy, and uncomfortable at first. I struggled to trust that the new way would hold. But just like my tennis swing, as I stuck with it, my faith grew stronger and more natural. I realized that letting go of long-held beliefs wasn't just an act of questioning; it was an act of faith. I wasn't abandoning truth; I was reaching for the One who is Truth.

> Letting go of long-held beliefs wasn't just an act of questioning; it was an act of faith.

Just like the woman who let go of her old ways of seeking healing, I had to loosen my grip on ideas that were no longer helping me and stretch toward the One who could truly make me whole. And now, on the other side of that valley, I know this deeper, sweeter, more intimate connection with my Creator was worth every moment of discomfort. I wouldn't go back to my former grip for anything in the world.

PRAYER

Dear God,

Thank You for walking with me through every season, especially the ones that feel uncertain and uncomfortable. You see the places where I'm still holding on to old ways of thinking or being, and You invite me to reach out to You instead. Help me let go of the grip that no longer serves me and embrace the new thing You are doing.

Guide me through the process of reexamining my beliefs, habits, and choices. Give me courage to release what is no longer true and to trust You with the process of transformation. Even when it feels awkward or clumsy, remind me that You are guiding my hands and my heart. I see through this encounter with the bleeding woman that sometimes healing is a partnership of my faith and Your power.

Thank You for being my Shepherd through the valleys. Thank You for loving me enough to challenge me and for leading me to a deeper, richer connection with You. May my life reflect a willingness to let go of what is familiar and reach for You, knowing that You are faithful to meet me there.

In Jesus' name, amen.

Reflect & Respond

Take time to process the following questions, inviting God to lead you. Revisit the examples shared in this chapter to spark your thoughts regarding yourself, others, and God.

Think of a time when a small shift in perspective led to significant change. How did that experience shape you?

What belief or habit have you been holding onto that might have served you for a season but now feels like a lid to your growth?

What fears come up when you think about letting go of old patterns or beliefs? How might God be inviting you to trust Him in that space?

What would it look like to invite God to help you regrip your thoughts, beliefs, or attitudes in this season?

Is there an area of your life that you are hesitant to reach out to God in faith? What is this hesitation costing you? What is one small step you can take to reach out to Him in faith today?

Chapter Nineteen

A Whole New "Well"

When we consider the healing of the bleeding woman, we see more than a physical miracle. Her encounter with Jesus transformed every part of her being—emotionally, mentally, relationally, and spiritually. Her story shows us that Jesus doesn't just want to treat symptoms. He desires to make us whole.

Twelve years of shame and suffering began to unravel as her fingers brushed the hem of His garment. The weight of isolation that had pressed on her soul for so long was lifted in a moment. Jesus didn't just heal her body. He restored her dignity. He silenced the lie that she was too broken to be loved.

We've already explored how shame (Chapter Four) and suffering (Chapter Six) shaped her journey and how they've shaped ours. Now let's turn to healing.

Shame makes us shrink back. It tells us we're unworthy,

unlovable, and too far gone. But shame cannot exist in the presence of Jesus. His love exposes and extinguishes it. When we step into the light of Christ, we are not met with condemnation but with compassion. In His presence, shame loses its grip.

Shame cannot exist in the presence of Jesus. His love exposes and extinguishes it.

It's time to release the shame. Jesus is not waiting for you to get it all together. Right now, He's extending His love. You are chosen. You are seen. You are enough, not because of anything you've done but because of who He is. He is enough for you and in you.

Here's a tender question: Do you believe that?

So many women bring their burdens to Jesus yet continue to carry guilt as if His forgiveness needs to be earned. But the truth is this: His grace is immediate. His healing is immediate. The *moment* the woman touched His garment, she was made well. And the moment you bring your wounds to Him, He forgives.

Let that sink in. You don't need to keep begging for what He's already given. Your next step is to receive it, to fully accept His forgiveness and extend that grace to yourself.

Forgiving yourself doesn't mean excusing the past. It means trusting His mercy more than your guilt. His sacrifice was enough. His love and grace are more than enough. You don't have to carry that weight anymore.

Let go. Walk in His freedom. "So now there is no condemnation for those who belong to Christ Jesus" (Rom. 8:1).

Jesus also wants to lift the weight of your sorrow. He knows what it's like to weep. He understands pain, grief, and loss. He sees your tears and knows the silent struggles you carry.

I am so sorry for the trauma and trials you've endured. But please hear this: You are not alone. Your Savior walks beside you, even in the dark. He does not shy away from suffering. He steps into it with you. "The Lord is close to the brokenhearted; He rescues those whose spirits are crushed" (Ps. 34:18).

Healing may not come in a miraculous instant, but Jesus promises to guide you, to hold you steady, and to remind you that your story isn't over. You still have a purpose. You still have hope. And He is with you every step of the way. "Then Jesus said, 'Come to me, all of you who are weary and carry heavy burdens, and I will give you rest'" (Matt. 11:28).

The woman in our story was also made well relationally. Jesus didn't just restore her body. He restored her ability to engage with others. No longer would she live in isolation. No longer would she be defined by the laws that once kept her hidden. She could now step into society, free to experience the beauty of friendship, the joy of laughter, and the strength of communal support.

Imagine that for a moment. After years of being unseen and untouched, she is finally welcomed. The door to connection swings open wide. She is no longer an outcast. She is invited in.

And love! What a possibility! No longer bound by

restrictions, she is free to build a life with another, to dream of marriage, a home, and a future filled with companionship. The very things that once felt impossibly distant are now within reach.

Jesus didn't just heal her; He restored her. He brought her back into the fullness of life, into community and love.

He is a God of connection and restoration. From the beginning, we were created for community, for meaningful, soul-nourishing relationships. Isolation was never His design. Love and connection have always been part of His divine plan.

Is this an area of your life in need of healing? What does God long to make well? Do you long for deep, life-giving friendships? Is God prompting you to open your heart to love? Or perhaps there is a relationship in your life that needs reconciliation, a wound that still lingers, a broken connection waiting to be mended.

Also, consider your dearest relationships. What intentional care could make them even richer and more life-giving? Perhaps it's making space for regular connection, choosing grace in moments of conflict, or expressing appreciation more often. Don't underestimate the sacred power of small, consistent acts of love. Text a friend. Make a call. Apologize first. Extend grace. Listen intently. These are the links that build deeper bonds and reflect Christ's love. Jesus is the healer of bodies and the restorer of hearts and relationships. Ask Him to guide you, bring the right people into your life, and soften your heart where healing is needed. He is able. He is willing. And He is already at work in you and through you. "Do all that you can to live in peace with everyone" (Rom. 12:18).

Finally, let's turn to perhaps the most profound healing in this story—the woman's spiritual healing. It's hard to grasp her view of God before her encounter with Jesus. She neither asked for nor caused her physical condition, but she was barred from entering the temple or even the outer Court of Women.

Don't confuse this with the modern, common view of church—something many may choose to attend if and when it's convenient and fits their schedule. For her, temple worship wasn't optional; it was *essential*. It was the center of spiritual life and identity for the Jewish people. Being cut off from the temple meant being cut off from communal worship, from the rituals that marked God's presence and in many ways from God Himself.

The woman lived in a culture that commonly believed physical suffering was the result of personal sin. She spent everything she had on doctors who failed to help her, and it's likely she also turned to religious leaders, only to face disappointment or even blame. Was she told her sin was too great? Her faith was too small? Imagine the weight of that spiritual shame. Her trust in both the medical and religious systems would have been shattered. Not only was she pushed aside by people, but she likely believed God Himself had cast her out.

Then everything changed in a moment. She received

healing power through His body, healing love through His eyes, and healing identity through His words. But it was more than that. It was sacred. There on her knees, something deep within her must have awakened.

She knew she was looking into the face of the Messiah.

In that holy moment, clarity flooded her soul. Everything she once believed about God was shattered. He wasn't angry. He wasn't distant. He wasn't the judgmental, elitist, unapproachable God she had been led to believe.

No, He was standing right in front of her—gentle, present, compassionate, holy.

This beautiful broken woman was granted the indescribable honor of seeing God face to face. While the crowd may have gathered to witness a man, she understood the truth—she had just encountered God in the flesh.

While the crowd may have gathered to witness a man, she understood the truth–she had just encountered God in the flesh.

In Chapter Eight, we reflected on the majesty of Jesus. Now we place ourselves on the receiving end of His glory. To deepen our faith, we must acknowledge that we all carry a limited human understanding of God, what I've called a Clay Chad perspective. As long as we live in these earthly bodies, we will never fully grasp the magnitude of who He is.

That's why we must constantly remind ourselves that He is bigger, better, and more loving than we can comprehend. He's never too busy and never out of patience or grace. He delights when we come to Him with expectation and awe.

I don't know what may have clouded your view of God. Maybe it was church hurt, unmet expectations, or the pain caused by people who misrepresented Him. If that's your story, you're not alone. Even those who've wounded us have their own limited view of God. We all do.

But here's the beautiful truth. Once your eyes are opened to His goodness, you can't unsee it. Once you've tasted His love and grace, no false representation can undo what you've experienced. He is better than you imagined, and nothing can diminish the depths of His love for you.

Once your eyes are opened to His goodness, you can't unsee it.

Spiritual healing is possible. Jesus isn't hiding from you. He longs for you to know Him more deeply and experience His presence in ways that transform your heart. Every doubt, every question, and every wound is an invitation to come closer.

Think about the times you've felt distant from God or confused about His nature. What life experiences may have shaped your view of Him? What have you misunderstood? Jesus is not put off by your questions. He welcomes them. He is here waiting to meet you with clarity, comfort, and love.

Healing begins when you open your heart to Him. Through His Word, prayer, and His gentle presence, He restores our view of who He is. He's not a distant or indifferent God but rather a loving Father, a compassionate Savior, and a faithful friend who walks with us through every season.

Let's tie all this together with a powerful truth from Scripture: "May God himself, the God of peace, sanctify you through and through. May your whole spirit, soul, and body be kept blameless at the coming of our Lord Jesus Christ." (1 Thess. 5:23 NIV).

This verse reminds us that God doesn't offer partial healing. He offers *wholeness*. He is the God of peace, not just calm feelings but shalom—a deep, holistic wellness that touches every part of who we are.

"Sanctify you through and through" speaks to God's desire to make us whole in every area—our spirit, our soul, and our body. Like the woman who reached for Jesus in faith, we are invited to reach for Him in our areas of need. His restoration isn't limited to physical health. It encompasses our emotions, our relationships, and our spiritual life too.

But healing is a partnership. God does the sanctifying, but we are called to participate and keep reaching for Him in faith. Sometimes healing is instant. Sometimes it's a process. And as we discussed in Chapter Twelve, sometimes it looks different than we hoped. But it always begins with trust.

So reach. Trust. Believe. Healing is available to you, not just for the surface wounds but for the deeply hidden ones too. God wants to restore you completely—spirit, soul, body.

And He's already begun.

PRAYER

Dear God,

Thank You for opening my eyes to the healing You so lovingly offer. You are a God who sees every part of me—mind, body, and soul—and You care too deeply to leave any part untouched by Your grace.

I can come to You without fear, knowing that You welcome me. Forgive me, Lord, for ever thinking that anything I've done could overshadow the power of Your love. Shame no longer has a grip on me. And I feel you in my suffering and find comfort in Your presence. You hold every tear I shed.

As I walk through these reflection questions, meet me in the stillness. Guide my thoughts, stir my heart, and reveal the places where You long to restore me. You promise that when I seek You with my whole heart, I will find You (Jer. 29:13). So here I am, Lord, with my heart wide open, ready to receive.

I can't wait to know You more, to trust You more deeply and to experience Your healing in every corner of my life.

In Jesus's name, amen.

Reflect & Respond

How have lies or misconceptions about God's love and grace hindered your spiritual growth? How does Jesus offer a new perspective on God's love?

Consider the woman from our Bible story. Our minds often focus on her struggles, but take a moment to view her through her strengths. There is so much to admire about this woman. Despite difficult circumstances, we can see that she possessed the following:

Courage
Trust
Resourcefulness
Perseverance
Power
Hope
Resilience
Curiosity
Focus
Faith

Now, pause and pray. Ask the Holy Spirit to reveal the positive characteristics you possess. Make a list. Pray over which one(s) you want to develop further. How do your strengths tie into your healing process?

God desires you to live whole and well in mind, body, and spirit. Take a moment to reflect on each of the areas below. Where do you sense a need for healing? What might it look like to partner with God as He restores you? Write out a plan, starting with small, attainable steps.

Physically
Emotionally
Mentally
Relationally
Spiritually

Chapter Twenty

"Go"—Stepping into Your God-Given Purpose

This verse wasn't just a farewell; it was a commissioning. The final words Jesus exchanged with the healed woman were laden with meaning. Her identity was now secure as His daughter, and she grasped the magnitude of her complete healing. Then He commissioned her to go.

We can only imagine her next steps, but one thing is certain. She didn't return to who she used to be. Jesus wouldn't have healed the woman only for her to shrink back in fear. He wanted more than her survival—He desired her full, abundant life.

Healing brings change, and change ignites purpose. She came to Jesus as a lost, desperate woman; she left as a new creation filled with hope, confidence, and peace (2 Cor. 5:17). A woman like that doesn't stay silent or still. She moves forward with a fire burning in her soul, ready to live fully and boldly. Jesus didn't just heal her; He sent her. And He is sending you too.

> Healing brings change, and change ignites purpose.

Jesus has called you out, and He's done so for a reason. You weren't created to remain stagnant, bound by your past. You, too, are a new creation. Healing is not just about freedom from something; it's freedom for something.

You've already demolished the walls you once hid behind. Fear of inadequacy or failure no longer has a grip on you. You're stepping out of your comfort zone, refusing to let lies hold you back. Jesus has called you out of the darkness.

Now it's time to boldly step into the light. It's time to confidently claim your purpose. You aren't just rescued; you are commissioned. The world needs the woman who's emerging. She's not tentative. She's not unsure. She's rooted, radiant, and ready.

Confidence in your purpose doesn't mean you have all the answers. It means trusting the One who does. Too often, we hold ourselves back, thinking we aren't ready to step into our purpose. But confidence isn't a feeling. It's a choice. And choosing to step forward in faith is how you walk into your calling.

We already spent some time in Chapter Nine with Ephesians 2:10. Let's come back to this powerful encouragement: "For we are God's masterpiece. He has created us anew in

Christ Jesus, so we can do the good things He planned for us long ago."

> You are His masterpiece, created with purpose, beauty, and intentionality.

When we think of a masterpiece, we often envision a work of art, something exquisite, unique, and irreplaceable. This is how God sees you. You are His masterpiece, created with purpose, beauty, and intentionality. But what does it mean for a woman to be a masterpiece in today's world?

Being a masterpiece means recognizing your intrinsic value and worth, not because of what you do but because of who you are—God's creation. It means understanding your uniqueness is part of His design and your voice, gifts, heart, and story are all part of His beautiful work. You are not a mistake or an accident. You were carefully crafted to fulfill a special purpose.

Think about an artist creating a beautiful piece of art. They don't just randomly throw paint on a canvas. Every stroke is intentional, every color chosen carefully, and every shape meant to communicate something unique. Artists don't hide carefully crafted works away in darkness. Similarly, God has painted your life with purpose. He has called you out for a reason. Your strengths, weaknesses, experiences, and challenges are all part of what make you who you are. And as a masterpiece, you are meant to shine in your own way. You don't have to compare yourself to others or try to fit into a mold.

You can step into your unique calling, whether that's

being a nurturing mother, a leader in your community, an artist, a teacher, or any role that is in your heart. When you embrace your purpose, you reflect the beauty of God's creation in ways only you can. For example, maybe you've been gifted with compassion. You can shine by using that gift to uplift others in your community, offering a listening ear or a helping hand when someone needs it most. Or perhaps you've been blessed with creativity. Don't hide your artistic talents or ability to think outside the box. Let them inspire others and point back to the Creator who gave them to you.

When you embrace your purpose, you reflect the beauty of God's creation in ways only you can.

You are God's masterpiece, crafted with intention and created with purpose. But embracing that doesn't mean striving for perfection. It means showing up as He designed you, using your unique gifts to shine for His glory. When you do, you fulfill the good works He planned for you long ago.

It's human nature to overthink this. Don't get so lost in pondering your purpose that you become stagnant. Consider a few practical steps to help spark momentum. Listen to God's voice. Spend time in Scripture, prayer, and stillness. Put pen to paper, journal about what stirs your heart, and discover what patterns emerge. God isn't hiding your calling. He's calling you out to step into it. Take time to listen.

As you seek His guidance, pay attention to your passions. What stirs your heart and brings you joy? Stay curious about circumstances that fill you. One summer, after returning from a beach trip with my church's high school youth group, I was physically exhausted but spiritually filled. I realized how much deep, personal connections and rich conversations about faith and life energized me. That spark led me to pursue a certification in life coaching, something I might have missed had I not paused to pay attention to what filled me.

> God isn't hiding your calling. He's calling you out to step into it. Take time to listen.

Notice your gifts and experiences. What do you enjoy doing, and how can past experiences influence your next steps? My amazing friend Stacy wrestled with her purpose when her family returned to the United States after serving as missionaries in Nicaragua for 10 years. She now serves as an English instructor at a local community college and delights in helping immigrant and refugee students obtain the resources they need to settle into a new country.

Sometimes our purpose unfolds in unexpected ways—ways we might not have chosen ourselves. Trust the process. God equips those He calls. Obedience starts with small steps, and the next step is always clearer once we take the first one. My beautiful friend Danielle felt a nudge to volunteer at Hospice. She told God, "Okay, I'll help at the front desk, but I won't work directly with patients. That would be too hard." But God tends to have a sense of humor, doesn't He? For over 15 years now, Danielle has been serving as a

Hospice volunteer who sits with families and patients as precious souls leave this earth.

Consider your life season. Your purpose will ebb and flow depending on your season of life. Stay open-minded to where God wants to use your gifts. Start with where you are. My dear friend Kristen has two sons in high school who play baseball. She knows their time under her roof will end soon enough, so you can often find Kristen on the ballfield. She's always loved photography, so she recently invested in equipment and enjoys taking high-quality photos of her sons and their teammates during games. Double whammy! She has discovered a dual purpose in supporting her sons' passions while giving back through one of her own. You don't have to wait for the perfect time. Your purpose starts where you are with what's in your hands today.

We must broaden our minds to the possibilities of our calling. It's easy to think of purpose in terms of a job title or ministry position, but God's call is so much more expansive. Your purpose might appear in the workplace, but it also flows through the roles you play at home, in your community, and in the everyday interactions with people around you. Your calling can shift and evolve with your season of life. What you're doing today may not be what you're doing 10 years from now, and that's okay.

Ultimately, our purpose is to make the name of Jesus known and do our part in advancing the Kingdom of God. That could be as varied as founding a nonprofit, offering a kind word to the grocery store clerk, rocking a baby to sleep, or leading a board meeting with integrity and grace. Your purpose isn't about one grand gesture, but a life lived with intention and obedience. There are countless ways to reflect Christ through who you are and what you do.

You have been called out of hiding, set free, and claimed as His daughter. Now Jesus tells you, "Go in peace" (Luke 8:48).

The order is important. What we do doesn't determine who we are. Who we are leads us to what we do. Jesus calls you His daughter, not because you've earned it but because He loves you. "You didn't choose me. I chose you. I appointed you to go and produce lasting fruit" (John 15:16).

You can do nothing to make Him love you more or less. His gift has set you free to go boldly into the world, to shine brightly. "In the same way, let your good deeds shine out for all to see, so that everyone will praise your heavenly Father" (Matt. 5:16).

You have been called out. "You are a chosen people. You are royal priests, a holy nation, God's very own possession. As a result, you can show others the goodness of God, for he called you out of the darkness into his wonderful light" (1 Pet. 2:9).

You are out of the shadows. Do not allow anyone, yourself included, to dim your light. The world needs what God has placed inside you. Your purpose is waiting.

Will you step forward?

The world needs what God has placed inside you. Your purpose is waiting.

PRAYER

Dear God,

Thank You for Your unshakable love for me. As I stand in this moment of revelation, I see Your hand all over my journey, guiding me to this point. You've revealed how I've hidden behind fear, insecurities, and doubts, and now You are calling me out to rise. I've received my true identity as Your daughter, and I declare this identity is the unshakable foundation of my purpose.

Forgive me, Father, for letting fear and comparison keep me stagnant, for allowing the enemy's lies to cloud the unique calling You've placed on my life. I repent for the times I've looked at others and thought their callings were greater or more important. But today, I proclaim this truth: My calling is uniquely mine, and no one else in the world can fulfill the specific purpose You've set before me.

I boldly declare my purpose is to shine for You. I will rise to make Your name known and advance Your kingdom with every step I take. Stir my heart, God, with an unquenchable passion for my purpose. Lead me forward, and I will follow, no matter how big or small the steps may seem. I surrender to Your guidance and trust You to direct my path.

Today, I take a step of obedience, knowing that with You, I can do all things. I will walk in the confidence of Your promises.

In Jesus's name, amen.

Reflect & Respond

Consider the fears, insecurities, and doubts holding you back. Imagine responding to Jesus's call while still carrying those excuses. How does that feel? What is it like to remain stuck in those fears? Now picture yourself stepping out, releasing those fears to Him, and embracing His call with faith and courage. How does that feel?

What sets your soul on fire? What brings you true joy and fulfillment? Think about those moments when you feel alive. What are you doing? What is it about those moments that speak to your deepest passions? What breaks your heart, and how might God use that to fuel your purpose?

How has God uniquely gifted you? Make a list of your best qualities and skills. Take time to reflect on the talents, passions, and abilities God has placed inside you. If you're unsure, ask a few trusted people for their insights. They may see things in you that you don't.

What is your next step in your purpose? Be specific. Write it out as a goal and give yourself a deadline. What tangible steps can you take today to move closer to the purpose God is calling you to? Consider resources, tools, or support you may need along the way.

Choose one of the verses in this chapter to memorize and recite when you feel stuck or uncertain. Declare God's truth over your life when doubt creeps in. Write the verse, keep it close, and speak it out loud as a reminder of who you are in Christ and the purpose He's called you to fulfill.

Chapter Twenty-One

Peace: The Final Word

In the middle of life's relentless pace—the never-ending to-do lists, laundry that seems to multiply overnight, appointments to make and keep, and the invisible burdens we silently carry—it can feel like a win to get through the day without a breakdown or snapping at someone you love. Chaotic circumstances often magnify our sense of inadequacy. In the exhausting effort to be everything for everyone, peace can seem like a luxury reserved for other women, the ones who appear to have it all together.

I can trace the path of my own life like a clumsy, crooked line in search of peace. Like so many in our modern world, I had accepted a watered-down version of peace tied to circumstances.

A little extra money in the bank.

No tension brewing at home.

A few quiet moments to myself at the end of a long day.

Sometimes I sought peace in a long walk on the beach as if it only existed somewhere far away, accessible only through escape. But those moments, while beautiful, were fleeting. They were not the deep, sustaining peace my soul craved.

We long for a version of peace that is more than the absence of noise or conflict. We want the kind of peace that settles deep into our bones, a steady calm—not just silence but a sacred exhale, a wholeness.

We want the kind of peace that settles deep into our bones, a steady calm–not just silence but a sacred exhale, a wholeness.

And in His typical way, Jesus raises the bar on the peace He offers. Peace isn't a temporary escape. It's not circumstantial. It's a gift. He wove this theme into mulitple unique interactions throughout His ministry, from His birth to His resurrection. When He entered the world, the angels declared "peace on earth" (Luke 2:14). When He returned after conquering death, His first words to His disciples were, "Peace be with you" (John 20:19).

The world's version of peace is very different. Jesus said so Himself: "Peace I leave with you; my peace I give you. I do not give to you as the world gives" (John 14:27 NIV). The peace He offers is deeper. Truer. Whole.

The Hebrew word for this kind of peace is *shalom*. It's often translated as "peace," but that barely scratches the surface. Shalom means wholeness, completeness, well-being, harmony across all areas of life—spiritual, emotional, physical, relational.

Shalom isn't the absence of struggle; it's the presence of fullness. It's when everything is aligned and your heart is at rest, even when the world is not. It's not perfection but integration, when your inner and outer worlds reflect the same peace. Nothing is missing or broken. It's life as God designed it to be.

This is the peace Jesus came to restore. In Isaiah 9:6, He is called the Prince of Peace, which is *Sar Shalom* in Hebrew. His mission was to comfort us and make us whole again. Shalom is what was lost in the Garden of Eden, and it is what Jesus came to return to us.

To live in shalom is to live in the nearness of God, as a soul that knows it is held. Even when the winds howl and the waves rise, we can say with full confidence that all is well, not because life is easy but because God is near.

Horatio Spafford knew this kind of peace. A successful lawyer in Chicago, he endured devastating loss. After financial ruin from the Great Chicago Fire in 1871, his four daughters drowned in a tragic shipwreck on their way to Europe with his wife, Anna. Only Anna survived.

As Spafford crossed the Atlantic to reunite with his wife, his ship passed over the waters where his daughters had perished. In his unspeakable sorrow, he wrote the words that would become one of the most beloved hymns of all time: "It Is Well with My Soul."

When peace like a river attendeth my way, When sorrows like sea billows roll;

Whatever my lot, Thou hast taught me to say, it is well, it is well with my soul.

That is shalom—Peace that defies explanation. Peace that doesn't erase the storm but steadies the soul within it.

With this deeper understanding, we return to the moment between Jesus and the woman who had been hiding for many years. "Daughter, your faith has made you well. Go in peace" (Luke 8:48).

Do you see it? That final word, *peace*, was not a simple farewell. It was a seal over everything Jesus had given her at that moment.

Wholeness.
Identity.
Restoration.
Purpose.

The woman reached out in desperation. Jesus responded with healing. And then He sent her forward with shalom, a renewed life wrapped in the presence of God Himself.

Peace wasn't something she had to chase anymore. It had found her. And peace has come for you too.

You're not the same person who first picked up this book, not after this journey with Jesus. Peace is no longer a fleeting or far-off dream.

Peace is within reach.

Is this a promise of a life of ease? No. True peace isn't found in the absence of storms but in the calm that anchors you within them. It's the deep assurance that you can bend without breaking, that you are resilient, held, and secure no matter what comes your way.

Peace is confidence rooted in identity, knowing who you are and whose you are. It flows from time spent with Jesus, from a relationship so grounded that fear loses its grip. What is there to fear when you're wrapped in the presence of the One who holds all things together? What could harm you?

Peace is confidence rooted in identity, knowing who you are and whose you are.

Peace is the assurance of an identity rooted as a daughter of the King of kings.

Peace is the unshakable belief that even when you can't see the way forward, God is still in control and working all things together for your good.

So maybe peace isn't just something we receive. Maybe it's something we choose to remember.

In Joshua 4, after God rescued His people out of slavery and led them across the Jordan River, He gave them a simple yet sacred instruction: Gather uncut stones—whole stones, complete and unbroken, ordinary yet chosen—and stack them high as a memorial, an altar of remembrance. When future generations ask, "What do these stones mean?" they would tell the story of God's power, presence, and provision.

You've crossed something too—a threshold from hidden to seen, from silent to speaking, from cast out to claimed.

This journey through the woman's story and through yours has been sacred ground. You've reached out in faith. You've looked into the eyes of the Prince of Peace.

And you've been called to go in peace.

So gather a stone. Find one that's simple and whole and place it where you will see and hold it often. Let it mark the healing God has begun. Let it remind you of all you've surrendered and all He's making whole and reclaiming. Let it speak of peace that no storm can steal.

This is your shalom stone.

May it whisper of God's faithfulness, your courage, and your story worth living.

PRAYER

Dear God,

Thank You for loving me too much to let me settle for a less-than version of the peace Your Son died to give me. Thank You for opening my eyes to the perfect, complete shalom You offer me. I invite Your peace into every part of my life.

Where there is chaos, speak calm.

Where there is fear, whisper truth.

Where there is striving, draw me into stillness with You.

Thank You for offering me a peace that doesn't depend on circumstances but on Your presence.

Give me the wisdom and courage to be a peacemaker in this world, by allowing Your peace to flow through me. May Your peace guard my heart and mind, reminding me of my true identity and purpose in You.

In the Name of the Prince of Peace, amen.

Reflect & Respond

How have you defined peace in the past? Has your understanding shifted after reading this chapter?

What areas of your life feel far from peaceful? How might Jesus be inviting you to trust Him there?

Can you remember a moment when you experienced peace that didn't make sense in light of your circumstances? What anchored you in that moment?

- *Activity:* There are many renditions of the beloved hymn "It Is Well with My Soul." Download one (or several) to keep close by. Let the words wash over you until they take root in your soul. Allow the melody and meaning to steady you in seasons of uncertainty and anchor you in God's peace.
- *Imagery Prayer:* Visual prayers can be powerful in centering your heart on Jesus. When anxious thoughts wake you or chaos feels overwhelming,

imagine yourself in a boat with Jesus. His voice and power speak stillness over the water, which looks like glass all around you. Take a few deep breaths and focus on the word *shalom.* When your mind drifts, gently remind yourself to stay in the moment with Jesus. Whisper *shalom.* Ask Him what He wants to reveal in your time together and how He wants His peace to guide the rest of your day.

Chapter Twenty-Two

Conclusion: Stepping Forward in Freedom

Through our journey, we've witnessed the woman's healing and the new possibilities that opened to her as she encountered Jesus. Yet she had no idea that their interaction was a foreshadowing of the greatest event in history. Take another look.

> There is breathtaking divine symmetry woven throughout this story.

There is breathtaking divine symmetry woven throughout this story. The woman who bled for 12 years, deemed unclean, barred from the temple, and unable to offer the required blood sacrifice, was ultimately *healed by blood.* But it was not the blood of an unblemished animal, not a temple offering. Her eternal healing was soon to come from the Lamb of God who would shed His blood on the cross.

The woman was barred from the temple. He was the temple.

She bled for years and was shunned. He bled for a day and was forsaken.

Her blood ruined her. His blood renewed her.

She reached out to touch not just His garment but the very temple Himself. Jesus was the fulfillment of everything the earthly temple symbolized—the dwelling place of God. Her outstretched hand didn't defile Him. Instead, His holiness flowed outward, covering her in healing, wholeness, and a new identity.

Before the cross, Jesus was immune to contamination—no sin or uncleanliness could touch Him. But on the cross, He chose to absorb it all. He took on her sin, her shame, her brokenness. He bore what should have made Him unclean so she could be made whole. And the same is true for you and me. "He was pierced for our transgressions, he was crushed for our iniquities; the punishment that brought us peace was on Him, and by His wounds we are healed" (Isa. 53:5 NIV).

Because of the cross you are no longer unworthy or unwelcome. You are healed, once and for all. "It is finished" (John 19:30). The Greek word for this phrase is *Tetelestai*, which signifies "paid in full." It marked the completion of Jesus's redemptive work, the debt of sin fully paid, the Law fulfilled, and the path to eternal restoration opened once and for all.

And the Good News continues. "But very truly I tell you, it is for your good that I am going away. Unless I go away, the Advocate will not come to you; but if I go, I will send him to you" (John 16:7 NIV).

As Jesus returned to heaven, He made way for His very presence to dwell within us through the Holy Spirit, our Advocate. And what is God's dwelling place called? A temple.

The woman in our story was banished from the temple. Then she touched *the Temple.*

Finally, she became a temple herself.

What she once longed to step into she became. Because of the cross and the resurrection, she—and we—are no longer barred from God's presence.

Instead, we are the very place where He dwells.

The story of this unnamed woman isn't just ancient history. It's your story too.

And now? You are healed.

You are seen.

You are free.

You are a temple.

So reach out. Stand tall. Walk forward, not in fear or hiding but as one who has been called, restored, and made whole.

> Walk forward, not in fear or hiding but as one who has been called, restored, and made whole.

You've been called out for good. The double meaning of this sentence is purposeful. You've been called out for good—permanently, once and for all, never to return to the shadows that kept you hidden. And you've been called out to *do* good. "Therefore, I urge you, brothers and sisters, in view of God's mercy, to offer your bodies as a living sacrifice, holy and pleasing to God—this is your true and proper worship" (Rom. 12:1 NIV).

And once again, we are struck by divine symmetry. The woman was unable to offer a sacrifice for her own healing. She was healed by the sacrifice of the Lamb of God.

And then she served as His living sacrifice.

Spending time as a witness to her story has strengthened my own.

The book in your hands is the result of my own journey through this powerful story in Scripture. I was walking through a season of spiritual dryness, feeling disconnected from God when deep called to deep. A longing stirred within me for a personal connection with Him, something more than routine or obligation. So I chose a few stories about Jesus to sit with intentionally, hoping to find fresh intimacy in sacred places.

As I lingered with this particular story, Jesus began to peel back layer after layer of His encounter with this beautiful, unnamed woman. The more I studied, the more I felt I knew her. And the more I knew her, the more I loved Jesus.

Not long after spending several weeks immersed in their encounter, I found myself at a David Crowder Band concert, hands raised in worship, tears streaming as the song "How He Loves" filled the room. As the music washed over me, scenes from the story began playing in my mind like flashes of light. And in that moment, it was as if that woman was right beside me, worshiping too.

I could see her clearly, eyes glistening with tears, face uplifted in awe and joy. I imagined glancing over at her, and in that sacred moment, we exchanged a smile, a nod of knowing gratitude—two women separated by time and bound together by the same healing love of Christ. It felt like closure. It felt like sisterhood. A quiet, holy solidarity formed not through shared circumstances but through shared transformation.

And now I imagine you too, another nameless woman to me but known to God.

It's my hope and prayer that as you've walked through the pages of this book and poured your heart into the entries of your journal, you've experienced a true breakthrough. It is my prayer that somewhere along the way, God's truth pierced through the noise and reached you at your core. I hope you've felt shifts, subtle or seismic, in your thoughts, your heart, your perspective. I pray that the weight of pain, fear, or insecurity has been lifted, and in its place you've discovered a deeper awareness of His goodness.

This kind of breakthrough changes everything. It renews your mind, removes false labels, and claims you—beloved, chosen, whole.

You've been seen. You've been restored. And now you've been sent.

Go forth not just as someone who was once healed but as someone who carries healing with her.

Let your life and your story echo the truth of the One who made you whole.

Let your life and your story echo the truth of the One who made you whole.

Let every step forward declare, "I have been with Jesus."

The story doesn't end when the bleeding stops. It begins when the silence breaks.

And you are not just part of this woman's story. You are continuing it.

It's the kind of transformation that demands to be shared and seen. The world is waiting for your voice.

BENEDICTION

My Beloved Daughter,

Take a deep breath. Feel My tender hands on your cheeks. Let My words take root in your soul.

I've been looking forward to this moment with you.

When your beautiful sister reached out in deliberate faith, everyone around her saw Me already on a mission, on My way to heal the daughter of Jairus.

But I stopped for her.

And I will always stop for you.

When sin feels overwhelming and shame threatens to smother your identity, reach for Me. I will stop for you.

When the ground beneath your feet shakes and the unthinkable happens, when grief crashes in, uninvited and heavy, carrying pain you don't know how to bear, reach for Me. I will stop for you.

When no one else sees your weariness, your wandering, your hidden tears, reach for Me. I will stop for you.

Beautiful daughter, keep reaching, even in the mundane.

In the quiet hours of the morning before you reach for your phone, your remote, or your to-do list, reach for Me.

When joy surprises you through a breathtaking sunrise, a kiss from someone you cherish, or a meal that delights your senses, reach for Me. I long to meet you there too.

I am not only the God who stops for the desperate. I am the God who walks with you daily.

I dwell with you in the ordinary. And I rejoice over you in your joy.

You are never invisible to Me. You are never too far gone.

You are never too much or not enough.

You are Mine.

While this part of our journey is coming to a close, it is only the beginning. Just as this woman's story has marked your heart, so your story will one day awaken another sister to My love.

So go in peace, in confidence, in purpose. You have a story to live.

You have a Savior who still stops for you.

Keep reaching, daughter. I will always be here.

With love,
Your Father

Respond & Reflect

Pause here.

Let these words settle into the deepest places of your heart. What is your Heavenly Father saying to you at this moment?

Write it down.

Let it mark you.

Let it remind you that you are never beyond His reach.

Respond in prayer.

"You will seek me and find me when you seek me with all your heart" (Jer. 29:13 NIV).

Acknowledgments

Michelle, my business partner and cofounder of Echo Joy Collective (EJC), this book wouldn't exist without you. Thank you for your obedience in tapping my shoulder in response to prayer. Your unwavering passion for God and His heart for women is inspiring and a constant fuel in my engine. I can't imagine this journey without you by my side.

Abby, from events to editing to dream boarding, your commitment to EJC and to all God has done (and will do) through our efforts have been a gift without a price tag.

Allison, your creativity, truth bombs, and insights have propelled us forward. I'm so grateful for the laughs and dreams we continue to share.

Danielle, our angel on earth, thank you for taking my words and applying your polish. Your constant smile and cheers have meant more than you'll ever know.

Kim, thank you for your brief but seismic comment: "I want in." Your hard work, input, and friendship keep EJC afloat in countless ways, and I praise God for you.

Stacy, your encouragement and support, both as an EJC teammate and a friend, have been a steady thread throughout my journey. You've talked me out of self-doubt more times than I can count.

To the entire EJC team, I pray God's blessings tenfold over all you have poured into this dream. I am so grateful for your faith, generosity, and belief in what God is doing through EJC.

To EJC, the beautiful women who preread this work, attended an event, or simply cheered us on, thank you for your trust and support in what God is creating through our efforts. Your feedback and your pom-poms have been wind in our sails, and your belief in the vision has meant the world.

To my tribe, you are my circle, my people, and my safe place to dream, laugh, cry, grieve, and grow. God uses our community to share a glimmer of heaven and remind me who I am in Him. I love you.

To my pastor, Jonathan, thank you for years of faithful shepherding and mentorship, and for the energy and thought you invested in offering feedback on this work. Your encouragement and insight have served this effort in meaningful ways. I'm so grateful.

To my beautiful family—Dad, my stepmom Sandi, Aunt Diane, Denise, and so many others—thank you for the love and encouragement.

To my boys, Jacob and Ben, being your mom is a joy beyond measure. Nothing has taught me more about the love of our Heavenly Father than walking alongside you. I'm so incredibly proud of you.

And finally, to my husband, Chad, you have a magical way of making me feel like I can do anything. Thank you for being my biggest cheerleader and my constant support. I love the life we've built together.

I am a woman blessed beyond measure and have been surrounded by some of the best people God has ever created. My cup spills over.

Appendix

Story Map

You have a story worth living. This resource will guide you through five simple yet powerful movements that will help you consolidate all you've experienced on this journey.

Each section represents a key part of your story, from the hidden places to the healing, and ultimately to the calling forward. Aim to be as concise and clear as possible, responding with one word or simple phrase. You don't need to answer every question; just choose at least one that resonates with you in each section. Allow the Holy Spirit to highlight the moments that matter most. This is not about perfection. It's about framing and sharing your voice.

Before: The Hidden Place

What were you hiding behind or hiding from?
Describe a time you felt stuck, ashamed, or unseen.
What lies were you believing about yourself, others, or God?
What did you long for, even if you couldn't fully name it?

Prompts:
I used to believe . . .
I was afraid that . . . Back then, I longed for . . .

The Turning Point: The Reach

What made you reach out to Jesus?
Was there a moment of desperation, clarity, or quiet prompting?
What gave you the courage to come closer?

Prompts:
The moment I reached for Him . . . What stirred my faith was . . .
Even though I was uncertain, I chose to . . .

The Encounter: The Moment with Jesus

When did you sense Jesus meeting you personally?
How did He speak to your heart or show up for you?
What did you begin to understand about Him and about yourself?

Prompts:
I realized Jesus was near when . . . He showed me that . . .
This moment changed everything because . . .

The Shift: Made New

How did your identity or outlook change after that encounter?
What healing (big or small) took place in your spirit, mind, or body?
How did your relationships, purpose, or faith start to shift?
How did your mindset, emotions, or sense of identity begin to shift?

Prompts:
Since that moment, I've noticed . . .
Healing looked like . . .
God is showing me I am . . .

After: The Calling Forward

What are you doing with your healing?
What do you want others to know about Jesus through your story?
How are you walking out your purpose now?
Who needs to hear your voice and your story?

Prompts:
Now, I believe . . . I am going to . . .
My story points to Jesus because . . .

Use this paragraph to consolidate your story:
I used to be ___________, but then I ___________. Jesus showed me ___________, and now I am ___________. Because of Him, I ___________.

As you complete your Story Map, remember that your healing wasn't just for you. It's an invitation for others to find hope too. Your voice is a vessel. Your story is a light in our dark world. Don't underestimate the power of your testimony in the hands of a faithful God. Whether you're still in the middle of your healing or walking confidently in your calling, your story matters, and it's worth sharing. Let this be your offering, your declaration, and your reminder that Jesus is still writing beautiful stories worth living, and yours is one of them.

(If you desire more resources or coaching support, visit www.echojoycollective.com and explore how we can walk through this together.)

A Note from Echo Joy Collective

A Story Worth Living is more than just a book—it's part of a growing faith movement to help everyday women live extraordinary lives by embracing healing, living with intention, and sharing their stories with boldness and grace.

This resource was created by Echo Joy Collective, and we've designed additional tools to walk alongside you on your journey. We invite you to visit our website to explore:

- Group facilitator guides to help you gather and grow with others
- Journals, coaching, and other offerings designed to help you make space with God in your life

Visit www.echojoycollective.com to discover what's available—and what's next.

We're so grateful to walk this sacred path with you.

With joy,
Amy Loflin & The Echo Joy Collective Team

About the Author

Amy Loflin is a widely regarded speaker, author, board-certified life coach, and cofounder of Echo Joy Collective. Combining an extensive background in counseling with over a decade in church leadership, Amy brings both expertise and heart to her work. She has served in multiple leadership roles, including groups director and serve director where she recruited and trained small group leaders, created on-ramps into authentic community, and partnered with local agencies to lead serve initiatives.

Throughout her career, Amy has enjoyed speaking to thousands of people from dozens of stages, including Forsyth Women's "Women on the Move Leadership Conference." She also served as part of her church's teaching team, where she delivered messages that encouraged spiritual growth and pointed people to Jesus.

A lifelong pursuit of Jesus has marked Amy's personal journey with healing, clarity, and contagious joy. Grounded in compassion, she has a deep understanding of the emotional and spiritual hurdles women face. Whether coaching, writing, or speaking, she has a unique gift for helping women move past what holds them back and live from a place of deep-rooted confidence.

Driven by the unrelenting belief that every woman has a story that is unique and cherished by God, she infuses her work with honesty, humor, and hope. Her relatable messages invite women to make space to dream bigger, live freer, and remember that wholeness and Jesus are always within reach.

Amy resides in North Carolina with her wonderful husband, Chad.

www.ingramcontent.com/pod-product-compliance
Lightning Source LLC
LaVergne TN
LVHW010611100826
845148LV00014B/2926

9781632968548